EFFECTIVE COUNSELLING

For Helen Anderson, my own Adlerian counsellor, whose life is dedicated to human potential.

EFFECTIVE COUNSELLING

A Groupwork Manual on Interpersonal Skills for Pastoral Teams

LYNX

Linda Smith

Published by
Lynx Communications
Sandy Lane West, Oxford OX4 5HG, England
ISBN 0 7459 2963 X

Albatross Books Pty Ltd
PO Box 320, Sutherland NSW 2232, Australia
ISBN 0 7324 1279 X

First edition 1995
10 9 8 7 6 5 4 3 2 1 0

A catalogue for this book is available from the
British Library

Printed and bound in Great Britain

ACKNOWLEDGMENTS

Every effort has been made to trace and contact
copyright owners. If there are any inadvertent
omissions in the acknowledgments, we apologize to
those concerned and will remedy these in the next
edition.

Scripture quotations taken from the Holy Bible,
New International Version. Copyright © 1973,
1978, 1984 by International Bible Society. Used by
permission of Hodder & Stoughton Ltd, a member
of the Hodder Headline plc Group.

Illustrations by Matthew Buckley

Note: The religious views expressed in this book in
no way reflect those of Alfred Adler.

CONTENTS

FOREWORD

Counselling is more important than ever in today's stressful world. All of us at some point in our lives take on the role of counsellor whether we know it or not. The very fact that someone has told you about her/his troubles and you have listened well, with interest and concern, says that you have already started.

At the time of writing there is no recognized association or government legislation which lays down rules for who can counsel and who cannot. There are many styles of counselling which all try to help people find new ways of coping with, handling or changing their daily lives. In this book I have chosen what I think are the safest and most useful of these many methods for distance learning. This book can be beneficial to the individual reader to help improve some of the skills used in daily life when communicating with people around us. It is also especially designed for use by home groups as a first stage to understanding the process of counselling and communication.

I have used these methods and activities while training Christian leaders— both lay and clergy. It is they who have repeatedly urged me to set their contents down in print for others to use. The skills work has also been used by student teachers on teaching practice who have found the skills gained from them invaluable when dealing with distraught pupils and staff, and in small group work for men and women who need to learn confidence and assertion.

This book is for anyone who wants to improve and refine her/his own relationships with other people. To do so requires thought and work and effort. A lot will also depend on a combination of your own natural ability and the level of your commitment to the task. But if you follow this course you will have the opportunity to increase your own self-awareness and improve your own human relations, as well as to practise how to help others do the same. In our world which is full of human conflict, hate, separation, divorce and interpersonal stress the challenge is on all of us to live differently and for the glory of God. May he grant us the energy and strength to learn the skill of human communication.

Linda Smith (Edwards)
King's College, London
May 1995

PREFACE

Here is a much-needed manual which enables individuals and groups, in both pastoral and community contexts, to find their way, step by step, towards greater self-understanding, a more assured ability to communicate clearly and the development of personal skills in helping others. It does not claim to produce the qualified counsellor (no book can!) but it offers an invaluable introduction to the essentials for more effective caring at every level. Like all good handbooks, the presentation is crystal clear. It is made up of six modules, each comprising three units. These carry the reader forwards in the learning process, through starter activities, groupwork, personal reflection and self-evaluation, laced with sharply observed case studies and challenging checklists on attitudes and behaviour. Linda Smith is an educationalist who has used this book's approach in a range of situations: amongst trainee teachers, with women and men who need increased confidence and assertiveness, and in training Christian leaders. She cites Jesus' model of caring for others as distinguished by humility and vulnerability. This user-friendly book opens up a way of living out this twin calling in the service of others.

Roger Hurding

Dr Roger Hurding is a counsellor and lecturer in Pastoral Studies at Trinity College, Bristol, and pioneer of counsellor training at Network in the same city. He has written a number of well-received books on counselling, notably the seminal Roots and Shoots.

FOR GROUP LEADERS

I have set out some guidelines for anyone who finds her/himself overseeing the counselling course or leading a homegroup on any occasion. You should read these before attempting the task because they will give you a context for the course as a whole.

WHO IS THIS COURSE FOR?

● Individuals who want to improve their own human relationships.

● Men and women who meet in twos and threes for social company but who want to do something more productive and learn better interpersonal skills together.

● Specifically for church housegroup study to equip lay people with counselling and communication skills.

THE CONTENT AND AIMS OF EACH UNIT

These are laid out at the beginning of each unit. Read these carefully as they are the focus of the whole session. When you have completed the work with your group evaluate whether these aims were met.

Each course unit contains:

● a starter activity;

● two or three group activities;

● a personal reflection exercise to be done at home; and

● a self-evaluation exercise.

THE SCOPE AND LIMITATIONS OF THE COURSE

Completion of this course **does not qualify anyone to be a counsellor** but it will mean that s/he has followed a recognizable course of study and practice to improve her/his own interpersonal skills. *Those readers who wish to pursue training can refer to the last unit for further reading and information.*

HOW LONG IS THE COURSE?

There is a suggested time given for each group activity, but the timing of exercises may be variable because different groups work in different ways. Therefore it is recommended that course coordinators read the unit before leading the session, and prioritize the activities to be done in the time available.

The course can be run in three different ways:

● Consecutively, unit by unit, in which case there are approximately eighteen weeks of work (six chapters with three units each).

● In stages: stage one as a course of six weeks (Modules 1 and 2); stage two as a course of six weeks (Modules 3 and 4); and stage three as a course of six weeks (Modules 5 and 6).

You may choose to run the stages at different times of the year. I do not recommend that you do the course over a period of more than a year because there needs to be recall of previous material and each set of skills builds on the others. Keep to the chronological order as far as possible because it is inappropriate to move to a high-order skill in Unit 5 before you have learned some basic skills in Unit 2. There is enough block material to learn stage by stage, and there should be enough time to digest it and work it through in between.

● By selecting one module of work to supplement existing programmes you are following with your group. You need to select the material carefully and check its validity, given the group's existing experience.

HOW DOES THE COURSE WORK?

Each module of this book is divided into three units. There is enough material in each unit to occupy a meeting of some two hours' duration. Obviously, not every group will have this period of time and there is no reason why a unit should be covered in every meeting. You may choose to do a unit over two or three meetings if you have time.

Alternatively, you will find that many of the activities can be done either in groups or as a personal reflection for each individual on her/his own.

HOW CAN I PREPARE FOR A COURSE MEETING?

Leaders should read the unit before the meeting and think through some of the following issues:

● **How the seating is arranged** so that course members can move their chairs and get into small groups.

● **How to introduce the evening** to show others that they know what is going to happen and to make them feel secure.

● **How the timing of the meeting is to be managed.** Most of the exercises need someone to keep time and to bring the group together. This can be done sensitively by:

■ Telling the group that you will keep time at the start of the activity or meeting.

■ Warning the group a minute or two before time is up that it has a short while to round up things.

■ Making sure that when members give their views, thoughts or feelings about what has been done, no one person dominates the discussion. Using a comment such as, 'Jeff, I'll have to stop you there as time is short but let's continue over coffee,' might be one way of doing this.

■ Realizing that occasionally a group member may be upset or disturbed by thinking about her/his own experience and preparing yourself mentally so that you have ways of channelling that person into a helpful situation. For example, be aware of the need to be with anyone who requires extra attention or to put that person in contact with trained professionals who can offer guidance.

COURSE THEORY AND GROUP ACTIVITIES

The theoretical material should be read by every participant but there is flexibility as to how many activities are attempted by each group. However, the course will not have the same results if there is insufficient time for activity work because it is there that we learn most about ourselves and others.

PERSONAL REFLECTION

You will find that in each unit there is a personal reflection activity for group members to do on their own. These provide them with opportunities to think through how the many issues we tackle affect their own lives. Course members might also like to use the personal diary pages at the end of each unit (see below) to keep a record of their own thoughts and reflections during the course. These can be invaluable to look back on and to assess one's personal development.

PERSONAL DIARY

There is a page at the end of each unit for group members to write their own personal diaries of the course if they so wish. This is intended for those who want to develop further their own self-awareness of how they respond and feel about the things they learn. Course coordinators may wish to give some hints as to how this can be done. If so any of the following may be helpful to focus on:

● Write in the first person using 'I'.

● Use the time to focus on your personal experience and development, not that of others.

● Explore your own personal relations with the rest of the group—the strengths and weaknesses.

● Ask yourself what you like and dislike about working in groups and think through how things could change for the better.

● Focus on the range of feelings you experienced during the session and afterwards. Be aware of your inner world and how it affects what you say and do.

● Think about the meaning of tonight's session for your own life. What are the personal things that need your time and attention at the moment?

Module 1

INTRODUCTION TO COUNSELLING AND COMMUNICATION

1.1 INTRODUCTION TO COUNSELLING AND PSYCHOTHERAPY

Think for a minute how much choice we have when we go to the local superstore. Nowadays it is not just a matter of buying a loaf of bread. We can have it sliced, unsliced, white or brown, granary or wholemeal, as a 'tin' or a 'batch', or maybe as a brioche—all bread, but in so many different varieties. The subjects of counselling and psychotherapy are similar; there is a wide diversity of approach and method currently available on the shelves.

At the start of this course we begin by asking the question 'What is counselling?' and looking at some of the answers that have been given. All approaches make assumptions, that is they (often) have unspoken beliefs about the nature of human beings and their goals in life. In this unit we look also at our own present assumptions about counselling and counsellors.

✔ AIMS

In this unit we have four aims:

- To clarify a working definition of 'counselling' for use in this book.

- To introduce you to three key theorists and to their approaches to counselling and psychotherapy, and to know and understand the assumptions they make about human nature and development: B. F. Skinner (behaviourism), and Freud and Jung (psychoanalytic theory).

- To increase your own self-awareness and to think through the strengths and weaknesses of the views you hold about the counselling process.

- To develop mutual understanding and deeper relationships within the group.

WHAT IS COUNSELLING?

If you ask anyone this question you will get a mixed response. Some people will accept the word counselling without any problem, others will want precise definitions of what is meant, and others still will have no confidence in this umbrella term which covers so many different and sometimes questionable practices. A working definition is important for us to have mutual understanding of what we are about. For instance, what is the difference between counselling and psychotherapy?

The table on page 13 illustrates the distinctions between different practices. (Based on R. H. Cawley's work referred to in D. Brown and J. Pedder *Introduction to Psychotherapy: An Outline of Psychodynamic Principles and Practice*, Tavistock, 1979.)

In this manual we believe that the appropriate level for those of us who are untrained is somewhere around level 1, possibly approaching level 2—depending upon our skill and sensitive understanding. A working definition of counselling, therefore, is a creative and supportive interaction between the person and counsellor which enables that person to clarify, reflect upon and consider her/his choices for action.

For those of you who are Christians this will, of course, also includes the view that counselling should help others to move towards behaviour, thinking and feelings which are in harmony with Jesus' teaching

Different approaches to counselling and psychotherapy

Counselling/psychotherapy 1

What any caring person, whether lay or professional does in supporting someone and encouraging her/him. This includes talking about problems to a sympathetic listener, expressing feelings within a supportive relationship and discussing problems with a non-judgmental helper.

Counselling/psychotherapy 2

The person is helped to explore at a deeper level. S/he looks at the causes of her/his personal problems. This includes challenging psychological masks, the defences we assume.

Counselling/psychotherapy 3

This is dynamic psychotherapy which probes unconscious processes. Usually this level is the domain of the experienced professional because it involves the phenomenon of transference in which the client transfers past experiences of a key person on to the therapist.

Counselling/psychotherapy 4

Where the client's problems are understood to relate to habitually bad behaviour, for example claustrophobia, and the aim is to help her/him relearn behaviour patterns.

and example. But in this manual we do not venture into the subject of spiritual counselling. Our aim is not to explore prayer, deliverance or inner healing, which are so popular in some churches today. Instead, we aim to help you equip yourself with the personal skills to enable you not only to counsel someone on personal matters but also to enhance your own personal communication at every level.

STARTER ACTIVITY (8 MINS)

In groups of two or three look at the following sentences and discuss between yourselves which are useful definitions and which are not. Share with each other any experiences you may have had relevant to any of these comments.

☺ **Counselling is all about giving someone the right advice.**

☺ **Counselling is about finding the right answers to people's problems.**

☺ **Counselling is being able to say the right thing at the right time.**

☺ **Counselling happens when someone in need finds there is someone s/he can go to who will have sympathy and share her/his problem.**

☺ **Counselling is about having someone older and wiser to go to.**

☺ **Counselling consists of having a skilled listener who can help you reflect on your own situation and who can open up the choices that are available to you.**

☺ **Counselling means digging deep into someone's past and helping her/him discover how the past influences her/him in her/his present situation.**

GROUP FEEDBACK (5 MINS)

One member from each group briefly reports back to everyone about some of the things discussed.

DIFFERENT THERAPIES AND METHODS OF COUNSELLING

Whatever approach you take to counselling, it will contain hidden assumptions about the nature of human beings, and the way they behave and live. We need to develop a thinking mind about these issues so that we can be enriched by the best of human insights and so that we can be discerning about what is clearly an inadequate view of human nature according to the teaching of Christ.

Three 'waves' have been identified in psychology:

● behaviourism;

● psychoanalytic theory; and

● humanistic psychology.

Here we look briefly at the first two 'waves' of approach to human growth and psychology: behaviourism and psychoanalytic theory.

BEHAVIOURISM

B. F. Skinner (1904–90) studied at Harvard University. He followed in the footsteps of John Broadus Watson (1878–1958) who was professor at Johns Hopkins University in the United States and founder of the behaviourist school. Skinner's theory of human behaviour is based on the concept of operant conditioning: 'When a bit of behaviour is followed by a certain kind of consequence, it is more likely to occur again, and a consequence having this effect is called a reinforcer' (*Beyond Freedom and Dignity*, 1973). These reinforcers can be either positive (if you tidy your room you get a treat), or negative (if your room stays untidy you get nagged). He attacks any view of human beings as 'free' to have internal states of knowing, will and destiny. Instead he states that consciousness is a social product. The desire for freedom is a response to negative reinforcement. For example, an overbearing

mother, rather than creating the desire to be free, may trigger a young person to leave home. In contrast, Skinner says that the experience of a sense of dignity arises from positive reinforcement. A teenager who is praised for her/his exam results will almost certainly repeat her/his efforts to succeed again. According to Skinner, a human being is simply a higher animal and man is a machine: 'Man is much more than a dog but like a dog he is within range of scientific analysis' (*Beyond Freedom and Dignity*).

GROUP ACTIVITY 1 (8 MINS)

QUESTIONS FOR GROUP DISCUSSION AND REPORTING

Get into groups of two or three people. Select one person to take notes for group feedback. The group discusses the following:

● 'We are all behaviourists in the way that we bring up our children.' Do you agree with this point of view?

● How would Christians (a) disagree and (b) agree with a behaviourist approach?

● Can you see behaviourism being useful to the way people counsel?

GROUP FEEDBACK (5 MINS)

Those selected feed back the comments of their groups to everyone. What are the similarities and differences between the groups' responses?

PSYCHOANALYTIC THEORY

SIGMUND FREUD (1856–1939)

Freud was born in the town of Freiberg in Moravia. His father was a Jewish wool merchant and following the rise of anti-Semitism the Freud family left Freiberg in 1859 (when Sigmund was three). They finally settled in Vienna in 1860; Freud lived there between the ages of four and eighty-two. Two of Freud's major discoveries were:

- the unconscious; and

- the Oedipus complex.

THE UNCONSCIOUS

Freud believed that neurotic symptoms were caused by buried memories. He later came to believe that hysteria and its symptoms were a result of traumas or emotional shocks received in childhood. People forgot or repressed the shock but the shock did not then disappear. Instead, it surfaced unconsciously in obsessive habits or bodily symptoms. Through psychoanalysis these traumas could be traced and dealt with. Freud believed that the unconscious shows itself in jokes, in errors and in slips of the tongue but, more than anything else, in dreams.

For Freud, dreams were a kind of code. If you cracked the code, you could find out what the problem was and set about curing it. Dreams were a combination of 'the residues of the day' (what had been happening) and repressed wishes (unconscious desires). Freud came to see the structure of the human mind as made up of:

- **The ego, the conscious self:** obvious everyday personality.

- **The *id*, the unconscious self:** repressed desires and memories.

- **The superego:** society's standard of morality forced on to a person from the outside and by which a person lives.

GROUP ACTIVITY 2 (10 MINS)

DREAM DISCUSSION

- **What does the group think of dreams?**

- **Are dreams 'the royal road to a knowledge of the unconscious activities of the mind'? As a group,** pool your own experiences of dreams. Are there any dreams which have helped you, or given you an insight into your self?

- **Discuss Freud's belief that buried traumas and repressed emotional shocks can cause physical and mental problems later on in life. Does anyone's experience in your group support or contradict this view?**

THE OEDIPUS COMPLEX

Oedipus was a character in Greek mythology who, unknowingly, murdered his father and married his mother.

Freud believed that male children are first attached to their mothers and see their fathers as rivals for their mother's love. (He later attempted to describe an 'Electra complex' for girls, but this was not so developed.) Feelings of fear and jealousy of a boy towards his father are mingled with a sense of guilt, as the child also has some feelings of love for his father. As a result of this early experience the child's sexual feelings are repressed until puberty when they surface again because of physical changes in the body. Freud claimed that a man's goals in life are to:

- detach himself from his mother;

- reconcile himself to his father; and

- find someone to love who is not identical to his mother.

One of Freud's discoveries was that childhood traumas are often sexual in nature. At first he believed in a 'seduction theory', according to which children had been introduced to sexual experiences at an early age. Later he came to believe that infantile sexuality operates at an age before people believed children could be sexual at all. His view was very controversial because many people wished to believe in the 'innocent', non-sexual nature of children.

Freud had no religious belief. He believed that religion is 'a universal obsession neurosis'. His work is still controversial, but it is also monumental. He stands as one of the great intellectual pioneers of the twentieth century.

CARL JUNG (1875–1961)

Carl Jung was originally an associate of Freud, but he broke away from him. Jung took Freud's discovery of the unconscious and expanded it. He believed in:

- **A personal unconscious:** this contains the repressed desires, memories and wishes of the individual.

- **A collective unconscious:** the reservoir of the whole human memory out of which myth and religion spring. All human beings share in the collective unconscious and are connected with it in some way.

- **Archetypes:** Jung treated the different parts of his personality as though they were different people and even talked to them. He believed that these figures exist universally in human consciousness and appear clothed in different forms at different times and at different places. These figures or symbols Jung called 'archetypes'. Archetypes occur in history, myth, literature and religion. They also surface in dreams.

Jung believed that dreams are creative symbols which have a meaning. They can tell us about the past or about the future. Their meaning, however, is not merely sexual, as Freud thought. Dreams are not solely neuroses in code. It is important to realize that an archetypal symbol cannot be explained rationally. When a person encounters one of these symbols s/he must respond emotionally and go on and on in finding meaning in that symbol without ever exhausting it. Jung identified four main archetypes:

- **The Anima (or Animus):** the mysterious female part of the male personality or the mysterious male part of the female personality.

- **The Wise Man:** the figure that represents wisdom, for example a hero, a king, a saviour.

- **The Shadow:** the dark primitive animal side of human nature. People often say 'I wasn't myself' or 'I don't know what came over me', when their shadow side gains control. Jung believed people have to learn to live with their shadow side in order to lead healthy lives. He was certain in his belief that there is no shadow without light.

- **The Child:** a symbol of wholeness existing in this world and the next. Jung believed that for a full life people have to live connected to the conscious and unconscious parts of themselves. The joining of these two parts in a symbolic whole is called 'the self'.

Society represses parts of the personality, pushing them down to the unconscious. Each person is forced to adopt a role and show a face, or mask, to the outside world. Jung called this the 'persona', named after the masks actors wore in ancient times. A healthy, balanced life, according to Jung, is found in someone who can give expression to all four main archetypes and who has learned to tolerate the opposites in her/his character.

GROUP ACTIVITY 3 (10 MINS)

Get into small groups of two or three. One of you, the recorder, should have a pen and paper.

- **Look at the Animus/Anima archetype.**

- **What characteristics are frequently seen as 'feminine' and 'masculine'? See if you can find three human** examples/situations where it is important for men to recognize and use their female side and for women to use their male side. Write these down.

● Look at the archetypes of the Wise Man and the Shadow. Can you think of biblical stories where these 'types' are important to Christians in their understanding of the faith? Write these down.

GROUP FEEDBACK (5 MINS)

Now the recorders feed back to the whole group and pool ideas for everyone's benefit.

Jung thought that the second part of life was far more interesting than the first part where sexual issues dominated. As an individual gets older s/he searches for wholeness and asks spiritual questions; s/he 'individuates', becoming much more her/his own person. S/he is established and settled but wants something more out of life. Jung realized that human beings are naturally religious and needed a myth or belief to live by. He felt that modern people are basically unhealthy because they can no longer believe in their myths and that they need to develop personal myths to survive. Jung came to believe that people need meaning and significance in their lives. Unlike Freud, who saw human neuroses as stemming from sexuality, Jung believed that sexuality was only a symbol of a higher spirituality. Humankind needs 'God' or else we will turn to creating idols.

The quest for meaning, for spirituality, Jung called 'individuation'. As the word suggests, individuation is the journey towards becoming a full individual. It is the quest to find 'God within' and the symbol of 'the self'.

In *The Secret of the Golden Flower*, Jung writes that when a person has undergone individuation:

It is as if a river that has run to waste in sluggish side-streams and marshes suddenly finds its way back to its proper bed, or as if a stone lying on a germinating seed is lifted away so that the shoot can begin its natural growth.

Jung spent many years studying alchemy, mythology and religious beliefs. Some found his work too mystical and obscure to take seriously, and blamed him for using evidence to fit his own theories. There is no doubt, however, that he was a man of extraordinary insight and sensitivity. There is more about Jung in Unit 4.3 where we look at his theory of personality types.

PERSONAL REFLECTION

According to Jung, individuation is the journey towards becoming a full individual.

● *On your own* find a comfortable place where you can work uninterrupted for ten minutes.

● On an unlined piece of paper draw a long twisting road to represent your journey as an individual. The road starts at birth and goes forward into eternity…

● First, plot all the things that you feel have helped you so far in your journey to become the person you want to be. Try to make them chronological. They might be diagrams or words and could include: books read, named people who have influenced you, videos/films, sermons, spiritual experiences and so on.

● Next, label what you think needs to happen in the future for you to fulfil your potential.

If you wish, you can use this exercise for personal prayer or share it with a friend in the counselling skills group and pray for each other.

SELF-EVALUATION

- Think for a minute about when you have counselled people and how you have approached this. What was effective and useful to people and what do you think could have been changed? Make a list of the changes you think are needed in your approach.

- What have you learned through this unit of work? What would you like to know more about and how can you start to find out?

- How did you feel relating to the rest of the group in this way? What were your feelings about the people you worked with? Did anything happen to make you feel that you belonged and were comfortable, or were your experiences different? What can you discover about yourself that would make it easier to understand your own responses in a group situation?

Personal Diary

1.2 HUMANISTIC AND TRANSPERSONAL PSYCHOLOGY

In this unit we look at the work of Eric Berne, Fritz Perls and Alfred Adler. All three men have expressed different insights and ways of helping people to understand themselves and other people. They are all optimistic about human beings, that is they all believe that with effort people can change and help themselves. In the next module we will look at another influential approach to counselling—the work of Carl Rogers.

✔ AIMS

The aims of this unit are:

● To expand your knowledge of different approaches to counselling.

● To give you the opportunity to try out and apply a variety of approaches to your own personal development.

● To give an opportunity for you to look at the different 'roles' you play in life (Parent, Adult, Child), and to assess how these roles help and hinder good relationships.

● To encourage readers who are Christians to think creatively and critically about secular practice.

ERIC BERNE (1910–70): TRANSACTIONAL ANALYSIS

Eric Berne said that all of us have three main aspects to our personality: Parent, Adult and Child:

● **Parent:** 'a set of feelings, attitudes and behaviour patterns which resemble those of a parental figure'. This can be either the *prejudiced Parent* where arbitrary values and prohibition surface, or the *nurturing Parent* who has sympathy and kindness for others.

● **Adult:** 'characterized by an autonomous set of feelings, attitudes and behaviour patterns which are adapted to the current reality'. The Adult in us is wise and thinks carefully.

● **Child:** 'set of feelings, attitudes and behaviour patterns which are relics of the individual's own childhood'. The *adapted Child* is dominated by parental control and may accept or withdraw, and the *natural Child* is independent, either rebelliously or creatively.

Desirable behaviour happens in complementary transactions. For example, a young man loses his job and shows that he is upset: 'I'm worried about the future.' His wife responds by hugging him and saying, 'It's all right, I believe in you, we can face this together.' His *natural Child* has appealed to her *nurturing Parent*.

Undesirable behaviour is caused by crossed transactions. For example, the wife asks her husband in a straightforward way, 'Will we have enough savings to go on holiday this year?' and is met with an emotional, 'Why do you always criticize me?' Her Adult question has activated his *adapted Child* which looks to his *prejudiced Parent*. Berne's popular book *Games People Play* (1964) sold more than 3 million copies. In it, he describes the transactions between people, or 'games', with clarity and humour.

Transactional analysis, or TA, states that we all have scripts and life positions which result from the 'decisions of childhood'. In this it relies very much on the earlier work of Alfred Adler. The aim of the TA counsellor is for the person to achieve a 'script-free' life in which s/he is aware of the games s/he plays. The astute counsellor can help a person to recognize her/his Parent, Adult and Child 'voices' and give her/him the option of choosing between these voices by 'discarding the non-adaptive, useless, harmful or misleading ones and keeping the adaptive or useful ones'.

STARTER ACTIVITY (10 MINS)

WHY DON'T YOU?—YES, BUT

- Below we quote from Eric Berne's book *Games People Play*. Join with a partner and read the game together out loud and then between you write your own 'Why don't you?—Yes, but' (WDYYB) script.

- According to Berne, what is the purpose of this sort of behaviour? Discuss between yourselves whether you agree with him? As a Christian what would you accept in his theory and what would you reject?

GROUP FEEDBACK (8 MINS)

Now join together with the rest of the group and share your scripts and your views. Can you think of any other 'games' that people play in their interactions with other people?

EXAMPLE OF SCRIPT

White: My husband always insists on doing our own repairs, and he never builds anything right.

Black: Why doesn't he take a course in carpentry?

White: Yes, but he doesn't have the time.

Blue: Why don't you buy him some good tools?

White: Yes, but he doesn't know how to use them.

Red: Why don't you have your building done by a carpenter?

White: Yes, but that would cost too much.

Brown: Why don't you just accept what he does the way he does it?

White: Yes, but the whole thing might fall down.

Such an exchange is typically followed by a silence and can be played by any number of people. The agent presents a problem. The others start to present solutions; a good player can stand off the others indefinitely until they all give up, whereupon White wins. Since the solutions are, with rare exceptions, rejected, it is apparent that this game must serve some ulterior purpose. WDYYB is not played for its ostensible purpose (an Adult quest for information or solutions), but to reassure and gratify the Child. A bare transcript may sound Adult, but in the living tissue it can be observed that White presents herself as a Child inadequate to meet the situation, whereupon the others become transformed into sage Parents anxious to dispense their wisdom for her benefit.

FRITZ PERLS (1893–1970): GESTALT THERAPY

Fritz (and Laura) Perls founded Gestalt therapy, which is concerned with the fragmentation in the human person and seeks to bring about an integration of the whole person. Perls wrote that the aim of Gestalt therapy is 'a unitary functioning of the whole man'. For the individual to 'come together', s/he has 'to heal the dualism of his person, of his thinking and of his language'. Gestalt emphasizes the 'here and now' experience and discourages reference to the past. The Gestalt counsellor or therapist acts as a catalyst for change. There are four phases in the process:

- **Expression:** the person, in our example a woman, is encouraged to express herself 'as fully as she can'. While she is so doing the therapist comments on her facial expression, breathing, tone of voice and so on. There may, for example, be a high tone of voice when talking about her mother. This present tense awareness should lead to differentiation.

- **Differentiation:** the person is encouraged to experiment and differentiate between the parts of her inner conflict. For example, the counsellor may suggest that the high tone of voice be exaggerated. In doing this, the client may realize that she wants to shout at her mother.

- **Affirmation:** the person is encouraged to identify with 'all the parts' that show themselves. She may say, 'I am my voice and I'm angry!' At this point the Gestalt counsellor will allow the person to express fully repressed emotion. This release can be very powerful. Perls said: 'Despite conventional notions to the contrary, this is the healthy device by which the organism exteriorized frustrated aggressions' (*Gestalt Therapy*). Gestalt is famous for the 'empty chair' technique where, after having expressed her feeling towards her mother, the woman in our illustration might sit on the chair and voice her mother's response to her own anger. She may then begin to get insight as she finds herself speaking for her mother: 'I'm glad you've been honest at last, I'm so weary of all your depressions and moods'.

- **Integration and choice:** during affirmation there can be an increase in self-awareness, an integration in which the person says, 'I am responsible for how I've been feeling.' Here the woman is encouraged to make choices about the insights she has acquired. She may choose to confront the situation, to rehearse the language she would use or to explore her own fears of expressing anger.

GROUP ACTIVITY 1 (10 MINS)

WHAT DO WE DO WITH OUR ANGER?

In groups of two or three explore ways in which people manage anger. Which of these is familiar to you? Which of these do you think is the healthiest way? Would you add any to the list? What consequences are there? Can you be spiritual and still express anger? As a Christian which of the following is most appropriate in loving your neighbour as yourself?

- Get angry but say nothing (*the anger stays within*).

- Get angry and avoid the person from then on (*the source of anger is avoided*).

- Get angry and express it there and then (*the feelings are shown and open to comment*).

- Get angry and blame the other person (*the anger is dumped elsewhere*).

- Get angry and go away and think about how to respond (*the anger is managed temporarily*).

- Get angry but transfer it from the person you are angry with to someone else who is easier to confront (*the anger is transferred, sometimes unknowingly*).

ALFRED ADLER (1870–1937): INDIVIDUAL PSYCHOLOGY

Although a follower of Freud, Adler broke away from Freud's ideas. Adler believed in the human power of choice rather than predetermined biological impulses. He believed that people can always choose how to respond to their inherited qualities and to the environment in which they grow up.

BORN TO BELONG: COMMUNITY INTEREST

The Adlerian view is that everyone is born with a desire to belong: to the family, to larger groups, to society and to the world. Everyone is also born in an inferior position and strives to overcome feelings of inferiority by compensation. For example, the boy who is small in stature could compensate for his sense of inferiority by striving in athletics, in body-building or in wielding positions of power over others. The girl who feels ignored in contrast to her sisters may strive to get attention by being ill, by being badly behaved or by retreating to her own private world and feeling superior in it. If their striving for superiority takes place in the context of social interest, that is with a mind to the interests of the whole of the groups they belong to, then there is benefit. But when children continue to feel inferior to others and unsure of their place in the world, their potential is severely limited.

GROUP ACTIVITY 2 (10 MINS)

THE ROOTS OF INFERIORITY

- **In a small group of two or three people read the case study on page 24.**

- **See if any of you can identify with similar events which made you feel inferior.**

- **Acquire a large piece of paper; one of you draw the trunk of a tree and give it ten long, wide roots.**

- **Label the tree 'Inferiority' and then as a group make your own list of some of the most damaging things that are said and done which make people feel inferior. Write these things inside the roots.**

GROUP FEEDBACK

One person from each group reads the list out to everyone. What are the things you all agree on? What can be done about these?

If you are reading this alone, you may wish to identify people who suffer from inferior feelings, and who need prayer and support.

SELF-EVALUATION

In a quiet place allow yourself to recognize your own levels of inferiority and then, in diary form, write what you feel and think about these. When you feel ready, share this with a counsellor, with a member of the pastoral team or with God. Ask yourself: *How could things be different?*

LIFESTYLE: THE PATTERN OF HANDLING LIFE

Adler would say that a person's basic concept of herself and her life provides a guiding line, a pattern that is fixed: this is called the **lifestyle**. The lifestyle is developed by the time you are five or six. Parents and the home environment are the raw material for children to begin to make some assumptions about themselves, the world and their chosen direction of how to manage inferiority. The ideas and beliefs upon which a person acts and functions are called private logic. Private logic is your own biased view of your own experiences, in contrast to common sense which is a view of things shared by the community. Individuals create their own unique lifestyle, and are therefore responsible for the development of their own personality and behaviour. This means that as human beings we are creative in manufacturing our own fiction about ourselves rather than being passive recipients of what others do to us.

EARLY RECOLLECTIONS AND MEMORIES: THE CLUES TO SELF-UNDERSTANDING

Adlerian counsellors help their clients by recording their earliest memories and identifying the purpose of their behaviour. This requires a certain amount of 'insight'. Adlerians think that when people gain 'insight' into their own neurotic behaviour and its purpose they are in a better position to act differently, and then change can happen.

THE FAMILY CONSTELLATION

This relational picture of a family is an important concept in Adlerian counselling. It is reflected, for example, in the following case study.

CASE STUDY: JILL AND HER SISTERS

Jill, aged thirty-eight, wanted counselling. The problem she presented was that she found herself unable to develop the confidence that she needed to form personal intimate relationships. For years she had thought herself 'ugly' and inferior to other girls—although she had a good figure and was physically attractive.

The Adlerian counsellor collected information from Jill about how she 'saw' her family when she was a child:

- Mary and Desmond were married and had five children, all girls, in quick succession.

- Jill was the first child and by the time she was one she had a baby sister.

- Jane was born number two in the family and Jill remembers her as a lively tomboy, the family favourite.

- Lucy was born number three, eighteen months later. Jill remembers her as ill-tempered, with lots of anger and force to her character.

- Dora was born fourth, a year later. Jill saw her as an affectionate, very loving, very feminine girl. By this time Jill was nearly four and all the children shared one bed in a one-bedroom flat, with their parents sleeping in the lounge.

- Elizabeth was the youngest, born two years later when Jill was nearly six. She was mentally disadvantaged and needed extra special care. As a result she got more attention than anybody else in the family.

Jill can remember at age three feeling displaced and 'dethroned' and less preferred. She got the impression that she was ugly because her mother and father were always complimenting the others for their looks and achievement, and she felt that all the attention in the family went elsewhere. She remembered vividly one occasion at the age of seven when all the sisters were dressed in their best clothes for Easter Sunday and she overheard her mother say to her father: 'They all look lovely, except Jill. She's the ugly duckling of the family.' Jill froze inside. She remembers feeling ashamed of herself, as if she was letting the family down. She quickly fell ill and had to stay at home. From that moment on she coped by becoming an excellent reader and spending long periods of time on her own. Her comfort was to live in a fantasy world of stories where girls were beautiful and things were happier. She hated attention being focused on her because she felt inferior and the best response was to hide.

Through careful research and attentive listening, the counsellor was able to help Jill to recognize the mistaken notions she had of herself. Even if she was the ugly duckling of the family she had a choice in the way she responded. She was not less valuable and she had other ways of responding to her early life than the avoidance strategies that undermined her confidence as an adult.

Adlerians would consider that a behavioural change is superficial if it is not accompanied by an alteration of perception and an increase in social interest. If people do not feel equal to others then real change has not occurred. In contrast, people whose mistaken notion is that they must always be the centre of attention, who rely on their own 'superiority' or 'specialness', are no more healthy than shy reclusive ones. They are concentrating on what can be given to them (self-absorption) rather than what they can give (social interest).

PERSONAL REFLECTION

Reflect on the above case study. Jill overheard something that she believed to be true—that she was less attractive than her sisters—and therefore she assumed that she was less valuable. To avoid inferiority she retreated from the public world into fantasy situations. This was her way of compensating. She was still doing it at age thirty-eight. Here are three possible responses that she could have made at the age of seven:

- **She could have overcome the inferiority by excelling at sport—all might have been well until old age or some accident prevented her from compensating in this way.**

- **She could have set out to please everybody—which might have worked until she started getting bullied at school and later on in her marriage.**

- **Instead, she decided to opt for control. She would control her own environment by limiting herself to**

literature and excluding people as much as she could.

To continue your reflection:

- **Pick a personality trait or perceived behaviour which you have been aware of for some time, either from the following list or something else which reflects your own experience:**

  - **Always trying to please people.**

  - **Feeling stressed because you cannot change plans when you need to.**

  - **Seeing relaxation time as laziness.**

  - **Allowing people to control your movements—when you eat, what you wear.**

  - **Feeling very angry when somebody says something you do not agree with.**

  - **Feeling stressed when people do not work or stay together.**

  - **Feeling guilty because you are not spiritual enough.**

- **Be as honest as you can with yourself. Think back and see how often this pattern has occurred. Give yourself plenty of time. Go back as far as you can remember and see if you can remember a time when you did not have this behaviour.**

- **See if you can pinpoint an incident in your own childhood memory that ties in with this behaviour.**

- **How did you feel when this incident occurred? With your new adult knowledge and your Christian faith, go back to that event and create a different option for yourself. Instead of the old behaviour, explore other possibilities.**

- Write down two other responses that you would now make and see how they would have affected your behaviour for the better. If you find this difficult or distressing on your own, then seek to share it with a counsellor or with God in prayer.

If you want to be a counsellor, receiving counsel and helping yourself by working on your own development and change is a very important part of the training.

SELF-EVALUATION

- What did you find interesting in what you have studied in this unit? Make a list of your interests.

- What was difficult to understand? Think of two questions you need to ask in the next session.

Personal Diary

1.3 JESUS AS A MODEL FOR COUNSELLING AND COMMUNICATION

In today's world, the non-Christian helping professions of counselling, psychotherapy and social work are necessary for the ongoing welfare of our society. As we have seen, there are many approaches which have contributed powerfully to people developing their own psychological and emotional health. For Christians there is, however, something more to draw upon.

In this unit we invite you to think further as a Christian about the nature of the counselling process. We look at what a Christian theology of counselling might include, by taking specific events and teaching in both the Bible, and in the life and ministry of Jesus, to guide us in our thinking and practice.

✔ AIMS

The aims of this unit are:

- To give you the opportunity to think as a Christian about the nature of the counselling process.

- To explore some of the methods of Jesus' ministry.

- To develop theological thinking about counselling and pastoral work.

THINKING IN A CHRISTIAN WAY ABOUT COUNSELLING

The life and ministry of Jesus as recorded in the four gospels provide Christians with a framework in which to develop their own counselling skills. Here we explore four different theological perspectives which have

relevance to the way a Christian thinks and works as a counsellor.

- **The incarnation:** God as person.

- **Jesus:** a model for human communication.

- **The forgiveness of sins:** a healing process in the ministry of Jesus.

- **The atonement:** the cross, evil and guilt.

THE INCARNATION: GOD AS PERSON

At the centre of Christian belief is the coming of God into the world in the person of Jesus Christ. Every Christmas we sing about it:

Veiled in flesh the Godhead see
Hail the Incarnate Deity
Pleased as man with man to dwell
Jesus our Emmanuel
From Hark, the Herald Angels Sing, C. Wesley, *1743, G. Whitefield, 1753, and others*

The overwhelming implication of this event is that God is personal. He came in Jesus Christ. John expresses it: *'The Word became flesh and lived for a while among us… full of grace and truth'* (John 1:14).

But think for a minute of the wider implications of the incarnation. God comes to us. God is one of us. Christ is equal with God but he empties himself and, in humility, takes the form of a servant, being born as a frail human being (Philippians 2:7). And this brings us to two themes which are crucial for the basis of all counselling done by Christians: **humility** and **vulnerability**. Let us explore these two attitudes by doing some group work.

STARTER ACTIVITY (10 MINS)

HUMILITY

How would you recognize humility in a counsellor? Get into groups of between two and four people. Your task is to write a dialogue between a quiet, depressed man/woman who comes to a counsellor for help. This is the initial meeting of twenty minutes to explore the person's needs briefly and to set a future time to meet for counsel. In your script, think through how you can genuinely express an attitude of humility by:

- The language you use.

- The questions you ask.

- The information you give about yourself.

- The suggestions you make.

GROUP FEEDBACK

If there is time, the groups can read out their different dialogues so that everybody can benefit from each other.

GROUP ACTIVITY 1 (8 MINS)

VULNERABILITY

Vulnerability includes taking personal risks, and showing people something of your inner thoughts and feelings. Professional schools of counselling are unanimous in their view that you cannot counsel well until you yourself have undergone self-examination. This exercise is an opportunity to increase your own self-awareness and to take risks in letting others in your group get to know you better.

You can do the exercise individually or you can get into groups of two or three. Discuss which of the following you find easy or difficult and, if you can, explore why that may be:

- Telling someone you are at fault and that you are truly sorry.

- Expressing your feelings of disappointment when someone has let you down.

- Sharing your feelings of doubt and difficulty in your Christian faith.

- Going to someone else for help.

GROUP FEEDBACK

Each person is invited to say something about how this exercise felt. Was it enjoyable, interesting, risky, challenging?

JESUS: A MODEL FOR HUMAN COMMUNICATION

It is easy to look at Jesus' teaching without thinking about his personal relationships with those he taught. As Charles Kraft has said: 'We look to Jesus for his message not for his method' (*Communication Theory for Christian Witness*, 1983). For the Christian counsellor, the crucial question is not only what Jesus taught but how he did it. How did Jesus teach and heal?

JESUS STARTED WHERE PEOPLE WERE AT: WITH THEIR FELT NEEDS

It was typical of Jesus, when he encountered individuals, to start not with the principles of his teaching but with a person's felt need.

GROUP ACTIVITY 2 (10 MINS)

- Read the following passages in the Bible and discuss amongst yourselves what Jesus said and how he acted according to a person's needs. Pay particular attention to Jesus' value of the person. What effect do you think this had on the person concerned?

  - Zacchaeus the tax collector (Luke 19:1–10).

  - Blind Bartimaeus (Mark 10: 46–52).

■ The widow of Nain (Luke 7:11–17).

● Think of someone who you have met or have known, and whose values and behaviour are unacceptable to you. Now imagine yourself in the position of being asked to help this person to improve her/his life. Think of three ways in which you could show your acceptance of this person (not her/his behaviour). What could you say? What could you do?

JESUS HELPED PEOPLE TO RAISE IMPORTANT QUESTIONS THEMSELVES

Jesus led his disciples to wrestle with questions rather than simply providing the answers for them himself. Answers that come too easily have little value. Jesus respects his disciples as learners, and good counsellors are the same; they do not give advice or have a ready solution, but they encourage people to learn deeply through their own processes. There are numerous illustrations of this method in the ministry of Jesus, for example:

● Jesus challenged his disciples to discover who he is (Mark 8:27–30).

● Peter is left to discover Jesus' words to him on the beach (John 21:15–19).

THE FORGIVENESS OF SINS: A HEALING PROCESS IN THE MINISTRY OF JESUS

... unless you forgive your brother from your heart...
Matthew 18:35

... and if he repents, forgive him...
Luke 17:3

Jesus said, 'Father, forgive them, for they do not know what they are doing.'
Luke 23:34

'Take heart, son; your sins are forgiven.'
Matthew 9:2

'Which is easier: to say, "Your sins are forgiven", or to say, "Get up and walk"?'
Matthew 9:6

At the heart of Jesus' teaching is the forgiveness of sins. In the gospels it is linked with healing and wholeness as in the story of the paralytic in Matthew 9:1–8 and Luke 5:17–26. In the Lord's Prayer, it is central that Christians forgive others and that God forgives them. Forgiveness reconciles God to people and people to each other. When someone is hurt, wronged or treated abusively, s/he harbours strong feelings about the person who did this. Secular counsellors help their clients by getting them to unlock their feelings, to express them or to replace them by choosing to respond in a different way. They may even help them in accepting that such feelings are part of their history and in integrating them in the rest of their life. All this can be essential to the helping process. But a Christian view goes further because Christ goes further. Christ commands his followers to change fundamentally the dynamic of bitterness, resentment, hurt or hate by interrupting the system and forgiving from the heart. For Christians and non-Christians alike the process can be a catalyst for change. But there are many superficial views about what forgiveness is.

GROUP ACTIVITY 3 (10 MINS)

Use the following as stimuli for thought. Discuss them with a partner and complete them:

● Forgiveness is more than just saying you're sorry, it's when...

● Some of the most common things that need forgiving in our community are...

● A person can't really begin to forgive until s/he...

- The process of forgiving someone else has to include these important things:

- Forgiveness is not easy because...

- Forgiveness can have powerful effects, for example...

GROUP FEEDBACK

Feed back your answers to the larger group and take notes on any differences in reply.

GROUP ACTIVITY 4 (15 MINS)

- True forgiveness and acceptance has an effect. Arrange the sentences below in order of priority. In your opinion, what are the most beneficial effects of forgiveness? Can you add any more to this list?

  - Guilt loses its power.

  - Bitterness is uprooted.

  - Self-worth is restored.

  - Blame no longer rules.

  - The truth sets you free.

  - Love flows, fear flees.

- Now, with one or two other people, choose one illustration of forgiveness in your own life and share the effect that this has had on you. Each person has between three and five minutes to speak.

THE ATONEMENT: THE CROSS, EVIL AND GUILT

In order to think in a Christian way about any system of counselling it is necessary to ask how Christianity views the dark side of human nature: sin, evil and guilt. In Genesis 3 we meet sin for the first time as Adam and Eve choose to disobey God by breaking the one rule he has set

them. Biblically, sin is just that—selfishness or self-rule. For example, when our own children blatantly disobey us, it temporarily puts a barrier between parents and children. In the Genesis account of the fall of humankind, there were consequences to human action:

- Guilt and fear: '... *they hid from the Lord God...*' (Genesis 3:8).

- Self-consciousness: '"*I was afraid because I was naked...*"' (Genesis 3:9).

- Blaming others: '... *she gave me some fruit from the tree, and I ate it*' (Genesis 3:12).

At the cross, the good news of the gospel is that Christ redeemed humanity from the consequences of sin (separation from God). It is in this area of the human fall that secular systems of counselling and psychotherapy are often at odds with Christian approaches. For example, humanistic psychologists all stress that human beings are essentially good and, with help, can change themselves. Questions of personal sin, repentance, real guilt and individual responsibility before God are often ignored.

JESUS DID NOT HELP ALL WHO APPROACHED HIM

Read the story of the rich ruler in Luke 18:18–30. In this story, Jesus quickly recognizes that the rich ruler wants an answer from him rather than to change. Counsellors are very often asked similar questions by their clients: 'How can I get rid of this depression?'; 'What must I do to be a happier person?'; 'How can I change this bad habit?'. Sometimes this is a genuine question and people are willing to make the necessary sacrifices to achieve their goals. Like the rich ruler, others want a quick answer from the counsellor and are not prepared to pay the price of change.

To save them further pain and distress, it is important that they identify their own level of involvement in the counselling process.

Otherwise they will expect you to give them answers and when you fail to do so they will continue to believe that there is no help available to them. Many counsellors can get caught in the trap of trying to solve clients' problems for them.

Below is a group activity based around a true-life story which helps you to focus on asking questions which would help you to decide at an early stage whether someone who sought your help had the personal commitment they needed to pursue real change in their life.

CASE STUDY: LARRY

Larry was aged forty-four and an ordained minister. He went to see someone he knew had counselling skills who had known him for a long time. He had fallen in love with a Christian woman called Emma who shared many of his own interests and whom he saw as an ideal partner. He told Emma that he could not continue with the relationship because she was taking far too much of his ministerial time. This clearly distressed him and a few weeks later he was feeling the loss of the relationship. He approached his counsellor for help. Larry is at odds with himself. What he says does not make sense; he loves this woman, they have a lot in common and yet he says she takes a lot of his time.

GROUP ACTIVITY 5 (15 MINS)

- **Make your own personal list of three questions which would help you find out the level of Larry's enquiry. Is he genuine in wanting to know himself better or does he just want someone to make him feel better and agree with everything he says?**

- **The counsellor realized after two meetings with Larry that at this point in time he preferred to blame his partner and his circumstances, and refused to look at the real issues.**

Outline some of the responses you think it is best for the counsellor to make to Larry in suggesting that they terminate counselling

- **Jesus skilfully overcame the avoidance strategies that people create to escape change. Jesus gave the rich ruler something to do. What would you ask Larry to do in order to see if he really means business about sorting this relationship out?**

- **Read the story of Jesus and the woman at the well (John 4). What difficulties did Jesus overcome in helping her to get to the real issues at stake? Here is a list of some strategies people can display to avoid the real issues:**

  - **Avoid talking about themselves.**

  - **Try to control the conversation to make it go their way.**

  - **Use excuses for their behaviour.**

  - **Think everyone else is to blame for what has happened to them.**

PERSONAL REFLECTION

HOW DO YOU CHANGE?

Your view of the fall is very important in counselling others. Three beliefs are described below. Look at them and think through how they might affect the approach a person takes to counselling:

- *Every potential:* an optimistic view of human nature. Human beings are born good; only afterwards do they make mistakes and even then they want to do what is right. Counsellors with this view will put a lot of trust in the ability of the people they are counselling to change themselves.

● *No potential without God:* a heavy, pessimistic view of human nature. Humankind is totally corrupt. Every human problem is caused by personal sin and unless a person is 'redeemed' by God at his initiative, s/he cannot be helped. Counsellors with this view will rely heavily on God to change either the situation or the people they are counselling.

● *Some potential to search for truth:* a restorable view of human nature. Humankind has fallen short of the glory of God, and the image of God is marred but not lost completely. Although only Christ can make a 'new creation' and restore the divine image, people still have a capacity to respond whether they are Christians or not. Counsellors with this view will probably use a variety of counselling methods and also pray for God's help and initiative.

This is a personal thinking activity to bring out the beliefs that you have about:

● Whether human beings have the power to change themselves.

● Whether only God can change them.

● Whether a combination of the two is true.`

How you view this question affects the approach you will take with a person who comes to you for help. For example, people who believe that only God can effect change feel that for them only prayer can change the lives of people. Of course, prayer does cause change and is a crucial part of the helping process, but this book assumes that the reader believes that a person who wants to change has to use his own free will and make his own efforts, no matter how small they are.

For your reflection:

● Write down all the things in your life that you have had to change, for example your house, car, job, school, hairstyle, the church you go to, your boyfriend/girlfriend. Who effected this change? Who helped you?

● As an exercise to help you to decide which of the three beliefs about human change described above is nearest to your own experience, pick out a change that was difficult for you. Think about it. Why did you change? Do you know why it was difficult? Explore the reasons for your change.

SELF-EVALUATION

Evaluate your own responses to this unit by asking yourself the following questions:

● With what do I most agree in this unit of teaching and with what do I disagree? What are my reasons for this? Do I need to think further?

● As a Christian how would I go about counselling non-Christian people?

● Would I do it and just show my care and support for them, accepting them as they are without mentioning aspects of the Christian faith?

● Would I find myself unable to counsel them because they do not have the same beliefs as myself?

● Would I make it clear at the initial interview that I bring Christian beliefs and practices into the counselling situation?

● Some other view?

Does your view need changing or expanding?

Personal Diary

Module 2

PREPARING TO BE A COUNSELLOR

21 KNOW YOURSELF
WHAT YOU BRING TO COUNSELLING

Whenever you counsel or communicate with someone else, both of you bring various skills, characteristics, and past and present experiences to the task. This unit focuses on *you* and what you bring to the helping situation. Some aspects of yourself, for example your biological gender, you cannot change. Other aspects, for instance your listening skills or your friendliness, you *can* change. The self that you bring to someone when you seek to help her/him possesses both strengths and weaknesses. Skilled helpers are those who learn to understand themselves, their positive and negative points, and who work to overcome their limitations.

✔ AIMS

In this unit our aims are:

● To explore the values, attitudes, beliefs and assumptions you bring to the counselling situation.

● To identify your own habitual communication patterns and to assess their usefulness for the counselling process.

● To examine your motives for wanting to counsel.

● To explore your own responses to potential counselling situations where the values or behaviour of the client may conflict with your own.

STARTER ACTIVITY: YOUR PERSONAL BAGGAGE (10 MINS)

When you go on holiday you take your personal baggage with you. You may have a selection of clothes, shoes, medical supplies and so on. If you travel by air, your travel luggage is put through an X-ray machine which can tell you the exact shape of the contents. This activity looks at the different kinds of personal baggage—the assortment of emotions, feelings, thoughts, plans and concerns— that you have with you *at this moment in time*. Exercises such as this help you to be more aware of what is going on inside yourself. In counselling, this can be very useful because it helps you to distinguish accurately between what the client is feeling and what you are feeling yourself.

● Individually, get an A4 piece of paper and draw a piece of baggage. You don't have to be an artist! It can be any shape!

● Focus on yourself for a minute and then write in the baggage the assortment of personal things you have brought with you to this meeting or place (see diagram on page 37).

● Either keep your diagram for personal reflection when you are alone, or join with one or two others in the group and spend two or three minutes each sharing your baggage. This activity can help in getting to know people better.

People don't want to hear what I have to say

No good at public speaking

YOUR OWN SENSE OF WORTH

Some people find it difficult to admit that they lack confidence yet others show it very readily. Neither extreme is preferable in itself. For example, people who are always saying that they lack confidence or ability may be trying to manipulate their listeners to look after them. People who never admit to any need and always stress how capable they are may be struggling with great inner fear about themselves. When you set out to communicate with or counsel other people you will be giving some sort of message about your own value, that is how you value yourself as a person. Your level of personal confidence influences the messages you send to clients about their worth. Consider the case study of Sarah.

CASE STUDY: SARAH

Sarah was a sensitive and caring woman in her mid-thirties who was a successful teacher and who enrolled at a twilight course in counselling skills. The course started with real counselling in which the trainees had to counsel each other. After the first few weeks the supervisor of the course began to notice that when Sarah was in the counselling role she had a number of ways of eliciting her 'client's' approval. She would avoid asking questions which might clarify the situation in case they caused disapproval. She would try to

laugh and joke and make difficult conversations lighter so that the client 'felt' all right. In other words, she was controlling the situation. The client was not allowed to explore the real issues because the counsellor could not handle the risk of being rejected.

Sarah had low self-worth. She did not think that she could be liked for who she was, rather she held the inner belief that 'I must always have my clients' approval'. This led to over-sensitivity to cues of rejection and she always made sure that such rejection was avoided. The counselling really satisfied her own needs, not those of the person who sought help.

GROUP ACTIVITY 1 (15 MINS)

This activity requires sensitivity and confidentiality, but it is a very important task for anyone who wishes to help others.

● **Get into groups of two or three people.**

● **In the list below you will find a variety of fears and anxieties. Individually, spend five minutes looking through them and noting any that you have either had to tackle in the past yourself or that you are aware of in the present.**

● **Now join with the other person/people in your group. Each person has five minutes to share her/his perceptions with the other(s) in the group.**

● **If appropriate, this can lead to a short time of prayer for each other. Or you could write up your thoughts and feelings in the personal diary on page 43.**

FEARS AND ANXIETIES

☹ **Fear of rejection.**

☹ **Fear of failure.**

☹ **Fear of being seen as incompetent.**

☹ Fear of your own feelings being shown.

☹ Fear of the anger of those you seek to help.

☹ Fear of making decisions about what to do or say.

☹ Fears about not feeling good or holy enough.

☹ Fears about being found out.

☹ Fear of having to change yourself.

☹ Fear of failing.

YOUR ABILITY TO ACCEPT PEOPLE

Carl Rogers believed that if people are going to be helped they need to be able to express their feelings and come to terms with themselves within an atmosphere of acceptance. They need to feel valued, not criticized or judged. (For more on Carl Rogers see Unit 2.2.) Those of you reading this book are invited in the exercise below to explore your own responses to a variety of situations, all of which occur frequently for both Christians and non-Christians. The illustrations we give here are deliberate. They may not have happened in your parish or community but they do often happen, and there need to be Christians who are not thrown in their faith or shocked with horror because one of their number has 'sinned'. Everyone is subject to the problems of life; we need to be equipped with love, forgiveness and clear thinking so that we can support individuals and enable them to want to change their own situation.

GROUP ACTIVITY 2 (10 MINS)

● Get into groups of two or three people.

● Be honest with yourselves and discuss the following problems. How would you manage if someone came to you with these difficulties? This is not an exercise on how you would counsel but on what your own responses and feelings might be. What issues arise? What would you do? How would you show acceptance of the person? What might you feel yourself? When there is a difference in the values that you and the client hold, what strategies could you develop to be true to your own values and yet affirm the other person (not necessarily her/his beliefs and behaviour)?

■ A sixteen-year-old girl from your church is two months pregnant. No one knows apart from you whom she has chosen to approach for counsel. She wants your advice as to how to obtain an abortion without the rest of the church or her parents knowing. She is frightened of what everyone will say and that they will condemn her.

■ The minister of your church asks to see you in confidence. He is seriously thinking about leaving his wife and his three daughters, aged six, ten and thirteen, and moving in with the woman he loves who is a church warden (same parish) and fifteen years younger than himself. He has just told his wife and he is obviously nervous and in a high state of anxiety (consider Matthew 19:3–9, Luke 16:18).

YOUR MOTIVES

Motives are notoriously difficult to assess. It is very easy to fall into self-deception. Many people who begin to train to be helpers or counsellors do not examine their reasons for doing so. Motives can be either beneficial or harmful, but some are more useful and more honest than others. What are your reasons for wanting to help others?

GROUP ACTIVITY 3 (10 MINS)

KNOWING YOURSELF

- Get into groups of any size.

- Look through the list below and prioritize three different motives for discussion.

- Discuss each motive in turn. One of you should make notes to feed back to the whole group. Ask yourselves:

  - Why is this motive either harmful or beneficial in counselling?

  - What might the outcome of holding these motives be both for the counsellor and for the client?

MOTIVES

- 😐 I am concerned for the welfare of other people.

- 😐 I have the sort of personality that others warm to.

- 😐 I have been through and resolved so much pain myself that I want to use it to help others.

- 😐 I am competent and confident in how I communicate and I want to use these skills for the good of other people.

- 😐 I have problems myself and because I have them I don't think those I counsel will feel threatened. They will be able to identify with me.

- 😐 I think it is a Christian's duty to do good for others.

- 😐 I am at the age where counselling is probably a good thing to take up.

- 😐 I know my Bible well and I am strong enough to cope with the stresses of counselling people who have problems.

GROUP FEEDBACK

After ten minutes of discussion the whole group reassembles and one by one each subgroup feeds back its comments.

YOUR ASSUMPTIONS ABOUT GENDER ROLES AND SEXUAL BEHAVIOUR

In Western society there are psychological characteristics which have traditionally been seen as either 'feminine' or 'masculine'. Feminine characteristics have included gentleness, patience, sensitivity to other people's needs, tenderness, affection, dependency, nurturing and warmth. Masculinity has included ambition, logic, aggression, power and strength.

In his book *The Psychology of Interpersonal Behaviour* (1983), Michael Argyle writes on the theme of interpersonal communication. His research strongly suggests that there are a number of skills where females are more socially competent than males:

- sending body language;

- receiving body language;

- being warm and polite; and

- smiling.

However, he also says that the feminine gender defined in this way has its own set of problems, for example in:

- expressing anger;

- exerting independence;

- acquiring power and status; and

- making personal decisions (autonomy).

Similarly, the traditional masculine role has created problems for many men. In order to live up to expectations they are preoccupied with the need for success, power and achievement. In many cases, this has restricted them in showing the full range of emotions to their friends and partners.

Your beliefs about sexual and gender identity will influence how you behave in the helping situation. For example, if your views are traditional you may assess your clients differently according to whether they fit into the traditional roles you value. You may even think that the aim of counselling is to get them to fit into those roles. Or you may bring to the helping situation assumptions about the type of sexual behaviour that is right or wrong when people go out with each other, or when they are married. If a counsellor's view dominates a counselling interview, the client will receive little help. S/he may even be persuaded never to ask for help again.

The increasing amount of knowledge we now possess about physical and domestic abuse, sexual harassment and rape makes the examination of our sexual and sexist assumptions a very crucial thing. When we counsel, the people we help stand to be influenced by our deeply held views on sexual differences, gender roles and male/female expectations. Take, for example, the case study of Fiona and Geoff.

CASE STUDY: FIONA AND GEOFF

Geoff was a loving husband who lost his job and came to John, his Christian counsellor, for help. He was suffering from a lack of self-esteem and purpose. His wife Fiona, in contrast, was increasingly successful, having been recently promoted from her part-time job to become a well-paid professional. They had decided to change their former roles. Geoff was now staying at home and looking after the children while Fiona was out at work full-time.

At the initial interview Geoff confided in his counsellor that he was reaching an all-time low. He stayed at home all day, cooking, cleaning and looking after their two children (aged two and four). He had no friends nearby and his former workmates were all working. His wife did not return home until late. After six months of applying for jobs and being turned down he felt there was nothing he could do well. He lacked even the confidence to think that he could do a good job fixing the shower.

Instead of exploring the many issues that were involved here, or helping Geoff to plan his own strategies to enhance his confidence, John instead gave his own advice. The problem was clear. Geoff was the head of the household, his wife was not. Women were not meant to be the breadwinners. Men were not meant to be mothers. The solution was to reverse the roles again. Fiona should stop work or at least take part-time work and look after the children. Geoff would then be free to go on seeking work or to help in church ministry.

GROUP ACTIVITY 4

- **In groups of between two and four people, or individually, evaluate the advice John gave to Geoff in the case study above. What does the group think? Is this going to help him to enhance his own self-esteem or is it going to lead to more problems?**

- **What strategies might Geoff employ to increase his self-esteem?**

- **What practical help could the church give Geoff in his situation?**

- **Which of the following questions would you ask Geoff? Are there other questions you would prefer to ask and why? Identify three aims you would have in helping Geoff.**

- Does Geoff see work as valuable only if it is paid?

- How did he view his own mother's and father's respective roles when he was a child?

- As a family unit can they survive on his wife's new income?

- Does he see his own new role as skilful?

- Are there groups in the area that he could join to make friends with other mothers and fathers?

- Could Geoff bring himself to view cooking meals for his wife and taking care of his family as a part of providing for their needs equal to bringing in a wage packet?

- Does Geoff see this as being a permanent situation?

- Does he feel his masculinity is being depleted and, if so, why?

- How much would he have to pay somebody to do his job of home care if he was working?

- What benefits would he think his children derive from his spending more time with them?

YOUR VALUES

Throughout this book there will be an opportunity to develop a range of skills to help you to prepare for the counselling process. The following exercise is a preliminary activity to encourage you to identify your own values and to see how they influence your own communication with those around you.

PERSONAL REFLECTION

Look at the list below and see if any of these values, attitudes or expectations are important to you. Using the list or adding your own points, see if you can prioritize three values that you hold dear to your way of living.

- *Love:* appreciating others for what they are and not just for what they do.

- *Family life:* being part of a family and valuing parenthood.

- *Fairness:* treating everybody as valuable, irrespective of their status or position.

- *Honesty:* being honest and expecting everyone to be honest and fair with you.

- *Responsibility:* working hard and not shirking responsibility.

- *Autonomy:* valuing independence, thinking for yourself.

- *Friendship:* expecting to give and receive loyalty to/from your friends and family.

- *Convention:* valuing tradition, conformity and obedience to the church/community/government.

Now answer the questions below and apply them to your own life. You may wish to write up your own reflections on this exercise in your personal diary. Look at your list of three priority values in your life:

- What do you do when others ignore the values that are important to you? Can you think of a real illustration of when this happened to you. What did you do? What might you do now with hindsight?

● How did you acquire your values? To what degree are they your own or other people's that have been handed on to you?

● What are your attitudes to premarital sex, extramarital sex, casual sex, teenage sex, group sex, homosexuality? If you were counselling someone, Christian or non-Christian, who acted in complete contrast to your own values, how would you feel? How would you set about managing the situation? What options would you have available to you?

● Explore your own boundaries. Can you see yourself counselling people with different values to yourself? What could you manage and what would be very difficult or even impossible for you?

YOUR BELIEFS/WORLD-VIEW

Everyone who counsels has her/his own view of how the world works and her/his own beliefs about God and her/himself. Any committed Christian who decides to counsel or help somebody else has access to all the resources that come through knowing and experiencing the love of God in her/his own life. Whilst it is clear that not all Christians have the same views on how to counsel, heal or help other people, there are indications in the Bible that many of the early believers in the church used a wide range of resources to bring the gospel of healing and salvation to a non-Christian world. Preaching was only one of the ways this was done.

SELF-EVALUATION

Below are a number of incidents in the Bible which show where either counselling or healing took place.

According to the time you have available look up any or all of these and think what Christian resources were present and effective. What methods were used by those who were counselling and healing?

● The woman at the well (John 4:1–42).

● The sick man at Bethesda (John 5:1–15).

● Ananias and Saul (Acts 9:1–19).

Evaluate your own situation at present:

● What gifts and abilities do you think you have to bring to the counselling situation?

● Are there qualities you would now need to add to your personal resources? If so, how can you acquire these? Is there anything preventing you from developing yourself more fully? If so, how can this be resolved? What needs doing and who can help you?

Personal Diary

22 COMMUNICATION AND MISCOMMUNICATION

Every day there are thousands of messages being received and sent between people. Some of these are ordinary messages such as: 'Please pass the salt' or 'Hello, how are you?' Others are specific messages asking for information: 'Can you tell me the way to the market?'; 'What do you do for a living?' But there are other kinds of message which provide the levels of respect, love and friendship necessary to all good human relations. These are messages about ourselves—the kind of people we are, the values we hold, and our likes and dislikes. And there are also the messages we want to give to others so that they have the information they need about who we are and what we are about.

In all of this, the potential for misunderstanding is great. Think of all the times you or someone you know has been misunderstood. Think of all the tension and hurt that was generated because you were misquoted or others thought you had said something which, in fact, you had not said.

This unit is about how we send and interpret messages from others. The counselling process depends heavily on the helper having good communication skills. But any relationship can be strengthened and deepened if you are prepared to invest in improving your own clarity and in understanding how messages are exchanged.

✔ AIMS

In this unit we have the following aims:

- To explore what happens in the process of communication.

- To clarify what is meant by 'good communication'.

- To identify a range of ways in which people misinterpret one another.

- To help you assess areas of strength and weakness in your own communication skills and to identify your own goals for improvement.

- To introduce you to the work of Carl Rogers.

STARTER ACTIVITY (12 MINS)

INTERPRETING SIGNS AND SYMBOLS

As a warm-up exercise to focus on this unit try your hand at the following activity:

- **On page 45 you will find a number of non-verbal or minimum-worded communications. Alone or with a partner decide:**

  - **What each means.**

  - **What each item actually says to you.**

For example, GPO means General Post Office, but *what it actually says to me* is that I can buy my stamps or send my letter. To someone else it might mean a long queue!

- **Make notes on each item and be ready to exchange your meanings with others in the whole group.**

1. **1989 vgc hrw G reg M.O.T.**	11. **K J B**
2. **SL 2 K2 P2**	12.
3. H_2SO_4	13. **P - K2 Qkt - B3**
4. **LUCIANO** **L 22** **+ 8** **TYRES**	14.
5. 	15.
6. 	16.
7. 	17.
8. **112110-P SUMMER BREEZE A. Waters 8**	18.
9. **R.S.V. P.**	19. **2 recep, 3 beds, cloak, oilch orig features**
10. 	20. **A.S.B.**

Note the process that can go on when someone does not know what is meant by an item:

- **S/he guesses at something which looks or sounds like the symbol or abbreviation:** *when in doubt opt for familiarity.*

- **S/he gives her/his own meaning to the item:** *it is better to get some answer than to look silly or ignorant by not getting an answer at all.*

- **S/he misunderstands the item, thinking that it means something else,** *like words, symbols and abbreviations can have double meanings when they are used in different contexts.*

THE PROCESS OF COMMUNICATION

There are two different ways of understanding what human communication is: the **process model** and the **semiotic model**.

THE PROCESS MODEL

The process model is a traditional one and can be understood easily. Look at the diagram below. In this model, the sender encodes the message. If the message is spoken it will be a collection of words and statements. He then transmits them in speech and, as long as there is no interference, the receiver gets the message. Interference can be a distracting noise or a problem on the phone line.

This way of understanding communication is well known in many training systems. It emphasizes the words—that is, the message—that is sent. Ask anyone who has trained as a minister. S/he will most likely tell you that a lot of her/his training was spent interpreting words and verses of the Bible and practising how to transmit thoughts about the scripture in words that people could understand. Teacher training courses have traditionally followed the same route. They emphasize the content of the lesson to be taught, stressing that students should plan their lessons carefully so that the content is well taught.

THE SEMIOTIC MODEL

The word semiotics may sound strange, but it simply means '**the study of signs and symbols**'. A semiotic approach to communication theory looks very similar to the process model. There is still a sender and a message and a receiver. But this time the emphasis is different. Instead of emphasizing the message, this approach stresses *meanings*. The most important thing is that the meaning of the message is exchanged. You can encode your message as carefully as you like, and send it at great expense of time and energy so that transmission is very clear, but if the receiver interprets the message differently, that is, if s/he puts a different meaning on your words, then communication has not taken place. In fact, miscommunication may have taken place.

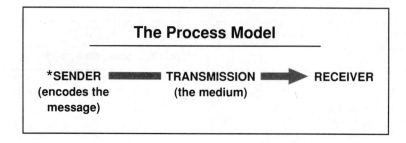

The Process Model

*SENDER ══════ **TRANSMISSION** ═══▶ **RECEIVER**
(encodes the   (the medium)
message)

Good communication occurs when there has not only been an accurate exchange of words but an accurate exchange of meanings.

COMMUNICATING SPIRITUAL MEANINGS

The difficulties of the communication process can often be seen when trying to exchange spiritual meanings. For example, consider the occasion when a very lively Christian youth leader spoke to challenge the local teenage population about what God was like. 'God is like a father,' he said, intending to assure everyone of God's goodness. Dave, a fourteen-year-old with tattoos and a scarred, shaven head, whispered, 'Well, I hope he's not like my father.' His own father had been imprisoned for brutally assaulting him when he was three. You may have heard this kind of story before but it is a simple and clear example of a single word, 'father', being taken in two completely different ways.

GROUP ACTIVITY 1 (10 MINS)

Below are two common phrases which people use and which are commonly misunderstood. As a whole group use the following material to stimulate thought and discussion about common misunderstandings. Does either expression have a standard meaning? Do you have any other examples you can share of incidents where the same word or phrase is used but completely different meanings are attached to it by both the speaker and the listener? Compare your response with others in the group. Were there any differences?

☺ 'I'M OK.'

Tick the occasions on which you have used the expression 'I'm OK.':

- You have had an accident, you have suffered injuries and you are asked how you are.

- You are offered a second helping of pudding/food but you are full.

- You have lost your wallet/purse and you feel very panicky; your friend enquires after you.

- You are sitting quietly looking serious. The person you live with wants to know how you are.

- You have suffered the death of a close friend or relative and other friends want to know how things are with you.

- Any other?

☹ 'I'M FED UP.'

Tick the occasions on which you have heard people use the phrase 'I'm fed up.':

- Someone has agreed to meet with a friend and s/he was let down.

- Someone has been accused of something s/he has not done.

- Someone has had a silly argument with her/his wife/husband/partner/parent/friend.

- Someone has just been told s/he has a serious illness.

- Someone has lost her/his door keys and is locked out.

- Someone has just lost her/his job whilst at the same time her/his wife/husband says they want a divorce.

- Someone is just feeling a little under the weather.

COMMUNICATING VALUES

CASE STUDY: JUDY AND MICHAEL

It is often the case that we do not realize what our own values and standards of behaviour are until they come into conflict with the values of other people. Take the example of Judy, a single woman who was a Christian and thirty-eight years old. She started going out with a Christian man called Michael who was her own age. Judy assumed that because they were both Christians and because they had a lot in common they would naturally find going out together a pleasurable thing. But early on in the relationship Judy found that Michael had very different values.

It was a small thing but it turned into a big issue. Whenever they would go into a restaurant or any public place where there was service, for example a shop or a cinema, Michael would treat the waiter or the supervisor as if s/he were worth nothing. There would be no 'please' or 'thank you', and no pleasant communication; rather s/he would get complaints and an attitude of contempt for her/his position. He *did not value* those whose job it was to serve him. This made such events stressful for Judy. She always felt as if she had done something really wrong. The issue was a very important one for her. Her embarrassment and concern for those who were treated in this way was obvious and it would irritate Michael. This difference in very basic values showed itself more and more as the relationship progressed and, despite both of them going for counselling, led to its eventual end.

Judy learned that you cannot even assume that Christians have the same values as other Christians. She also learned how important her own values were to her and that she could not sacrifice them even for the hope of a permanent relationship which she very much wanted.

Your set of values really makes up your own philosophy of life. What values are important to you? Counsellors are in a far better position to counsel if they are aware of the basic values they themselves hold. You may find yourself helping people with very different values from those you believe in, in a situation in which it may be possible to try to change them so that their values are more akin to your own. This cannot be called counselling for it seeks to impose or exercise change upon another person. For real change and development to take place, the person seeking help has to want it. S/he has to come to value things for her/himself. In the meantime the counsellor often has to value the client who may behave and speak in ways s/he dislikes.

GROUP ACTIVITY 2

YOUR WORLD OF VALUES

- Get into groups of two or three people if you are in a group, or work on your own if you are doing this course individually.

- Look at the list of values below. List any of those that are important to you, any that you disagree with and add any that are missing:

  - To treat all people you come into contact with as equal in worth.

  - Not to judge others as inferior because of their behaviour.

  - To be able to speak your mind without censorship.

  - To enjoy freedom of movement.

  - To respect each other's privacy.

  - For your effort and hard work to be recognized and affirmed.

  - To have the opportunity to change plans.

- **To be able to make mistakes without being rejected.**

- **To be able to respect someone without liking her/him.**

GROUP FEEDBACK

Reassemble as a whole group and, referring to your groups' lists, discuss between yourselves where these values have come into conflict with others. What was your response? Could things have been different? What did you learn from this situation?

The art of caring for and counselling people with whom you profoundly disagree in the basic things of life is a high-order skill. If you judge their behaviour critically it is almost certain that they will either terminate counselling or seek to avoid being criticized by not being totally open and honest. Thus the very qualities you need—honesty and trust— are undermined. The art is to accept and care for them unconditionally while at the same time helping them to focus on the dysfunctional behaviour or lifestyle which undermines their potential.

Learning to accept and value the people who come to you for help is a fundamental part of the counselling process. But it is not always an easy task. The psychologist Carl Rogers said that unconditional positive regard for the client was crucial. Without it, effective counselling would be impossible.

THE WORK OF CARL ROGERS: UNCONDITIONAL POSITIVE REGARD

Carl Ransom Rogers (born 1902) published his major work *Counseling and Psychotherapy* in 1942, and *Client-Centred Therapy* in 1951. These publications outlined his non-directive approach. This has several distinct features:

- The counsellor adopts an approach of non-interference by taking a **'low profile'** in the counselling process.

- By being a **facilitator** rather than a directive force, the counsellor allows the person in need to achieve insight into his or her condition.

- For this reason, all attempts at suggesting, interpreting, persuading, directing and pressurizing are ruled out because they obstruct real progress and change. It is a **client-centred** approach, rather than a counsellor-centred one.

- The counsellor's **attitude** is crucial to effective counselling. The counsellor must have genuine trust in the client and be able to communicate that s/he trusts the client's capacity to change at every level.

- **Trust** is powerful and it is communicated to the person who needs help by the counsellor's genuineness, unconditional positive regard and empathic understanding.

CASE STUDY: JOHN IN HIS MID-FORTIES

For Rogers a person is ready for counselling when his or her concept of self is at variance with his or her daily experience. Consider, for example, a married man in his forties called John who doubts his own worth and experiences a period in his life where his self-esteem is very low. He has once again been passed over for promotion and, at the same time, he is aware that his own personal attractiveness and zest for life is decreasing. Yet he finds that, to his surprise, he meets with approval and reassurance from his family and his workmates. They clearly show him that he has value. His own sense of worthlessness in conflict with the positive regard that others have for him brings inner conflict and, in time, he becomes very unsure of himself and seeks help.

By offering a client-centred approach the Rogerian counsellor helps John to restructure his own sense of who he actually is. The process may include some or all of the following stages:

- **Catharsis:** John is encouraged to **recognize and express his feelings** as they arise. By being able to express buried feelings, John becomes more relaxed and is able to look at his life objectively.

  John may find this threatening to begin with because men (and women) fear that such expression is unacceptable. The counsellor encourages him to express himself by communicating genuine empathy and warm concern for him.

- The counsellor creates a **'safe' climate of trust and acceptance**. He shows that his regard for John is unconditional, that is that he must know that he is valued no matter what he says.

- John finds himself experiencing **inner conflicts and inconsistencies**. This Rogers called the 'disorganization of the self'.

- **Insight:** when John finds that even his emotional distress is valued by the counsellor, he realizes that despite the fact that some of the worst is known about him he is **still valued as a person of worth**. The way is opened for insight where he can begin to form new perceptions of himself.

At the heart of the Rogerian approach are two points. First, the therapeutic value of the relationship between counsellor and client. The following quotation illustrates this:

... in my early professional years I was asking the question, How can I treat, or cure, or change this person? Now I would phrase the question in this way: How can I provide a relationship which this person may use for his own personal growth?
On Becoming a Person *(1961)*

Second, Rogers gave personal experience real authority in determining how an individual's life is to be understood. In *On Becoming a Person* he writes, 'Experience is, for me, the highest authority' and, 'No person's ideas, and none of my own ideas, are as authoritative as my experience.' It is not surprising that Rogers thought that one of the marks of effective counselling is an openness to all personal experience.

Carl Rogers' theories on therapy and counselling have been enormously influential in the counselling movement. His emphasis on the profound effects of what can happen when a person in need feels genuinely valued and accepted by a skilled professional is movingly reflected in this quotation about certain times in therapy:

... it seems that my inner self has reached out and touched the inner spirit of the other. Our relationship transcends itself and becomes a part of something larger. Profound growth and healing and energy are present.
A Way of Being (1980)

PERSONAL REFLECTION SELF-EVALUATION

Carl Rogers believes that giving unconditional positive regard to people is a powerful resource to help them work towards their own health and self-development. Think about how easy or how hard it is for you to do this. How can you develop this skill during the next weeks? Where and when can you put it into practice?

Personal Diary

2.3 HOW TO START
THE FIRST COUNSELLING APPOINTMENT

Many of you reading this book will have already started counselling others. If so, you will probably be aware of some of the initial pitfalls which may await the new recruit to the helping process. It is not unusual to find that in the enthusiasm of wanting to love, care for and help others the counsellor sooner or later experiences disappointed expectations, or even an acute sense of failure. Much or all of this can be avoided if, at the start of the process, there is a clear and realistic foundation laid between client and counsellor of what is being offered and what is not.

For example, a person may arrive at counselling with the unreal expectation that you, because of your reputation or her/his perception of your skills, can solve the problem s/he has in her/his marriage. S/he may expect you to intervene, to speak to her/his wife or husband and help her/him to see sense. Meanwhile your intentions are to help this individual to focus clearly on the personal issues at stake, and to come to a perceptive and thought-out decision. You may wish to pray with her/him for ongoing insight and courage. The expectations of client and counsellor in this situation are poles apart, and it is better to negotiate mutual expectations than to disappoint someone two months later because you either promised great things which have not materialized or because you cannot do what s/he expects. It is more desirable to work carefully and truthfully with the inner resources that both client and counsellor possess than to dig ditches and then fall into them.

✔ AIMS
Our aims in this unit are:

● To plan and role-play an initial meeting with someone who needs help.

● To draw up a list of the information you will need to counsel someone for any length of time.

● To help you to develop awareness of non-verbal communication and its effects.

STARTER ACTIVITY (10 MINS)
What do you look for in a first meeting? What makes you feel comfortable and open to talk freely? Sometimes you already know the person you are going to counsel—even so, the first time s/he comes for counselling is an important event for her/him.

● **Get into groups of three or four people and together look at the list below. Which of these points are essential when you go for a first meeting (or for an important meeting) and why?**

● **Individually, write down three things that you would add to the list from your own experience and then get together with your group again and share/discuss what you see as important.**

ASPECTS OF A MEETING

● **A genuine smile to greet you.**

● **An enquiry about what the journey was like or how your day has been.**

● **An offer of something to drink.**

● **Being shown where to put your coat or where the toilet is.**

● **Evidence that you are expected, for example that the table is laid for a meal or you are shown to a room that is obviously prepared for a discussion.**

THE INITIAL MEETING: NON-VERBAL ISSUES

The **location** of the meeting is important because it can help or hinder the level of conversation you need to counsel effectively. A room that is too dark, too hot or too draughty, or in which the phone rings constantly, will cause distraction. Ideally, you need privacy and quiet. If this is not possible you might be able use a deserted part of the church or maybe a friend can loan you a room for a while. Some good counselling has even taken place in transit, that is, in the car or walking round the park. Think through how and where you can offer the best environment.

You may see someone in her/his own home. This can tell you things about her/him which you may not otherwise find out from seeing her/him in your own environment. If you see people in your office or living-room it may be more difficult to control the timing of the interview. If you use your own home for the counselling session you need to arrange the seating so that both yourself and the listener are on equal terms. Avoid barriers between you such as chairs or desks. Interesting posters or pictures behind you can be a signal for the client's attention to wander off, especially if you are getting onto difficult ground.

SPATIAL AWARENESS

Spatial awareness is also important because what is adequate space for you may not necessarily be the same for someone else. One such issue is where and how you place the chairs in the counselling session. Many writers comment that both the position and the proximity of the chairs is important. Below are a number of chair positions for a one to one situation.

● **Position 1 (two chairs head one)** is considered to be too confrontational.

● **Position 2 (two chairs side by side)** does not allow you to see the other person easily and naturally.

● **Position 3 (two chairs at a two o'clock position)** looks unfriendly and disconnected.

● **Position 4 (two chairs at a four o'clock position)** is the one favoured in many schools of thought.

GROUP ACTIVITY 1 (15 MINS)

Sensitize yourself to the needs and requirements of others by doing the following activity:

● **Elect a timekeeper for the exercise.**

● **Arrange yourselves in twos; each person has a chair.**

● **Sit quietly without talking in position 1 and when time is indicated by the timekeeper (one minute) talk to each other for another half minute about how that felt.**

● **Move to position 2 and do the same exercise, then repeat it for positions 3 and 4.**

● Finally both partners in the pair move their chairs until they feel they have settled on the very best position. You should feel comfortable enough to talk together and to remain silent if need be.

SPATIAL PROXIMITY

Our needs for spatial proximity vary enormously according to both our moods and the level of intimacy we share with the person we are talking to. Have you ever had the experience when you are talking to someone at a social gathering that you suddenly feel as if you are too close to her/him (or too far away)? You move away (or closer) only to find a few moments later that s/he has moved closer (or further away) again. If this continues you can dance your way around the room in no time! If a client feels too close or too far away s/he will be concentrating on her/his own spatial needs and not on the questions that are important. It is worth asking the client at the initial interview if s/he is happy with the seating or whether s/he needs more or less distance. This way you can negotiate what is of mutual benefit.

GROUP ACTIVITY 2 (10 MINS)

● Get into groups of two. One of you is A and one of you is B.

● You will need some space for this exercise so you may have to use hallways, kitchens or other rooms for a minute or two.

● B positions her/himself in a static position a distance away from A.

● A then moves towards B and stops when s/he is comfortable.

● Both A and B stay in this position for about fifteen seconds and then change places.

● The next thirty seconds are spent together talking about the experience and negotiating what space would best suit the two of you together. You might like to join another group and show them your conclusions and compare it with theirs.

EYE CONTACT

As most people realize, eye contact is important. Counsellors all agree that too hard a stare for too long is threatening and confrontational. Looking away from the client for long periods of time can indicate non-interest or embarrassment. It is felt that the most appropriate model for eye contact in the United Kingdom is one of continual movement and interchange between parties. Both speakers should be in a position in which they can look at each other when they wish and also look away when required.

THE INITIAL MEETING: OBJECTIVES TO AIM FOR AND CONSIDER

Although every person, situation and task is different, it is helpful to think about what you would see as the most important objectives to be gained from a first meeting with someone. Here are four aims for this initial meeting:

● Developing a caring, supporting working relationship.

● Mutually agreeing the structure of the meetings.

● Defining a way of working together, discussing some of the processes to be used.

● Exploring personal preferences of time and location.

Having carefully thought-out aims has advantages. It can:

- Focus your session and give you and the client the security of knowing at least the outline of how things will go.

- Clear away unreal expectations of the counselling process.

- Help to set sensible targets and boundaries for the sessions.

- Record important information that both counsellor and client need to know about each other.

- Help you to determine whether you can begin to help this person or whether there are other support services s/he needs to be linked with.

It is important, of course, to allow some flexibility so that issues can be dealt with as they arise.

GROUP ACTIVITY 3 (15 MINS)

- **In groups of two read the following diary account by Lena.**

- **Designate yourselves A and B. A is the counsellor; B is the client.**

- **Clients on this occasion are to choose the same issue as Sue chose to discuss for a role-play: her mother's behaviour.**

- **Using the diary account as stimulus material role-play an initial interview. A should take the initiative from the start. The interview should be restricted to between ten and fifteen minutes.**

GROUP FEEDBACK

When you have finished, come out of the role by giving each other feedback on what the session felt like for you.

LENA: NOTES FROM HER FIRST MEETING WITH SUE

Lena is a counsellor who has spent time working out her own approach to counselling. Below are the notes from her first session with Sue. (*Note:* In this case study, Sue is not suffering from extreme distress and crisis. We will look at the management and handling of crisis in Unit 5.3.)

DIARY ENTRY FOR INITIAL MEETING WITH SUE WILLIAMS

�➤ *11th October 1995*

Sue was prompt and we started the meeting at 10:10 a.m. after preliminary chat, giving her coffee and showing her the bathroom.

➤ *10:10–10:20 a.m.* I explained to Sue what I saw as the purpose of our first meeting.

- To get the information we both need to record about times available for counselling, telephone numbers and necessary information for my records regarding whether she has been to anyone else for counselling, medical treatment and so on.

- For me to let her know what I could and could not offer with my knowledge and expertise, how I counsel and what she might expect.

- For Sue to give me information about the needs she has and the situation she perceives herself to be in.

I then asked her if she was happy with this approach and whether in the hour we had there was anything else she would like to add. She said that, as a Christian, she would value a short time of prayer at the end of the session and I readily agreed.

➤ *10:20–10.30 a.m.* We collected each other's working times and discussed possible venues. My place looked the most convenient and I can always put the answerphone on. We agreed this. I recorded that Sue had already been to two other counsellors and had met with little success. This led naturally to the next item on our agenda.

➡ *10:30–10:40 a.m.* I started by asking Sue what her expectations were in coming to me for counselling. She told me about her previous disappointments; that she had just been given verses of scripture to believe in and to have faith in. Nothing had improved. She wanted someone who cared about her enough to meet regularly, and to give her problems time and attention. I told her that I felt I could meet those expectations. What I could not promise was that we would automatically solve and relieve her stress. I told her that I would help her to identify and focus on some of the real issues at stake. This could mean some uncomfortable sessions for her and for me because I might have to confront lovingly her perceptions of herself. But all along it was her choices that were important if she was to change and develop. She was happy with that and I said that I would copy down all we had talked about at this stage so that we could both refer to it if we ever needed to re-examine our aims together or if we ever go off-track. I suggested that we both kept a personal diary of our times together to keep track of our thoughts and feelings.

➡ *10:40–10:55 a.m.* We checked the time we had and I invited Sue to talk to me about the kinds of things that were causing her stress. She told me about her mother whom she perceived as being highly manipulative and possessive. Although Sue lives away from home she is constantly at the beck and call of her invalid mother, who lives on her own and constantly accuses Sue of selfishness and of being just like her father. This leaves Sue drained and exhausted, and unable to live at peace with herself because she is getting so

angry. She also feels very guilty and every time she feels like this she wonders where to begin in getting rid of the guilt but it defeats her. Her previous counsellors had told her to honour her mother and to pray for her anger to go away. She might even need delivering from anger, they had said.

I let her talk and I assured her that next week we could begin to explore some of the events and feelings associated with her mother, and some possible ways of coping and developing from the present state of affairs. I assured her of the confidentiality of our meetings.

Our hour was up but I had time to check that Sue was happy with the session. She assured me that she was relieved to find someone who would listen to her and not butt in all the time. I said I might have to butt in sometimes if needed. We laughed, and we had a few minutes of prayer together to ask for God's power and guidance for our next session.

Next week I shall give her some homework to do, but I thought that quite enough had happened for one week.

PERSONAL REFLECTION

Read the diary that followed Lena's first counselling session with Sue. Spend time writing your own outline of what a first counselling session might look like. Your outline should include:

- **A breakdown of the time and topics you would introduce for mutual discussion.**

- **A checklist of the questions you would ask and the information you would need.**

SELF-EVALUATION

How do you come across when somebody first meets you? Here is a checklist of things to think about and to

do in order to evaluate how you present
yourself on first meetings:

☺ Do you smile?

☺ Do you say something positive?

☺ How do you hold yourself—are you
relaxed, nervous or reserved?

☺ What kind of eye contact do you
give: direct, indirect, avoidance?

☺ Do people feel comfortable meeting
you?

Ask a trusted friend who knows you in
different situations to comment on the
first impression you make.

Personal Diary

Module 3

DISCERNING WHAT OTHERS ARE SAYING

3.1 EXPLORING GUILT AND BLAME
THE WORK OF J. B. ROTTER

You cannot counsel for very long without discovering that one major source of psychological stress and anxiety is that people are undermined because they feel that they are guilty. Sometimes this can be something from a long time ago which has just been allowed to surface in their minds. Or it may be in the immediate past when they felt blamed for some act, a weakness or just for being the sort of people they are.

There are basically two ways that guilt and blame can be transmitted. One is from the outside, that is, someone tells us. We then have a number of responses we can make: reject it, receive it or weigh it up and consider it in the light of the person who said it. The second is from *within* us. For some reason we have inwardly decided that we are always to blame and that we are guilty. This can be harder to trace and sometimes harder to address, for the person who is long-suffering in guilt has already been convinced of her/his own liability and faults. Changing this view is often a process that takes place over a period of time rather than in a few counselling sessions. In contrast, some of you reading this book will be witnesses to the unconditional love of God in Christ which is, for the Christian, the most powerful and the most wonderful means of breaking the chains of guilt and blame. This can happen in a moment. Nevertheless, guilt and blame are not restricted to those outside of the Christian church—plenty of believers suffer just as much and for just as long. In this unit we look at a number of issues which relate to handling these problems.

✔ AIMS
The aims of this unit are:

- To increase your awareness of how much power you give to what others say.

- To identify some of the labels and comments that people have attached to you and to review your own use of language when describing others.

- To learn about and understand the work of J. B. Rotter and the 'locus of control' in our lives.

STARTER ACTIVITY (10–15 MINS)
How much attention do you give to what others say about you? You need a timekeeper for this exercise.

- **Look at the following questionnaire and answer the questions. Record which of the options reflects most closely how you would generally act (3 mins).**

- **Get into groups of two or three and discuss the options you have marked. Each person then has three minutes to talk about what happens in her/his own experience when events like these occur.**

- **Add anything to the list that you know is a specific issue for you. When you are alone think and pray about what other options you might have rather than accepting what is said.**

QUESTIONNAIRE:
WHAT POWER DO YOU GIVE
TO WHAT PEOPLE SAY AND DO?

1. You meet a friend who has not seen you for a long time. The first thing s/he says is, 'You've put on a lot of weight since I last saw you.' What do you do?

   (a) feel rejected and unattractive;

   (b) pass it off with humour;

   (c) consider losing weight if necessary.

2. Your boss/teacher/father/mother says something like, 'You'll never be any good at that will you? It's a pity you're not like (name).' Do you:

   (a) get upset and keep it inside;

   (b) get angry and protest;

   (c) get thinking and consider who has said it and for what reason.

3. You are not someone who finds it easy to talk about your feelings. Your partner/friend accuses you of not caring enough about her/him because you do not share your thoughts with her/him. If you were of this disposition would you:

   (a) feel inadequate as a person because you cannot please your friend/partner;

   (b) say that you thought the accusation was unjust or simply misplaced and blame your partner for her/his perceptions;

   (c) think about whether or not this is normally the case and see how you can prevent misunderstandings in the future.

4. You arrange to meet a friend/boyfriend/girlfriend/partner for an evening at your house at 7 p.m. You are still waiting for her/him to arrive at 7:40 p.m. This is the second time this has happened with the same friend. Do you:

   (a) feel demoralized that s/he has not bothered to turn up or inform you of her/his lateness;

   (b) phone her/him straight away and say that this is unacceptable to you because it does not value your time and commitment to her/him as a friend;

   (c) think through whether this friendship is worth the effort and then decide what to do.

If you scored all or mostly (a)s then you give a lot of power to other people to upset and discourage you. Think: is it worth it?

If you scored all or mostly (b)s then you simply reject what people say to you without too much thought. Think: what do you gain and what do you lose with this behaviour?

If you scored all or mostly (c)s you put effort into evaluating what has been said to you and looking at the long-term issues. Think: you are already thoughtful and creative in your responses. But be careful you do not think too much about things that are not worth it.

THE LABELS THAT STICK

Some people go through life as if there is a label stuck to them. These labels are the statements that other people have made about them. They can be labels about how able you are, how good- or not so good-looking you are, or they may give a verdict on your morals or criticize your values. In fact, labels can be about almost anything. As long as they are verbal judgments about a person they are labels.

Some labels can be good. These are the springboards of life which launch us into creative and productive activities. Take, for example, the teacher who told an unconfident fourteen-year-old that his ability for writing essays was exceptional; they were the best he had read in years. This label read: 'You are exceptional.' That teenager went from strength to strength. The label had a life-long effect on him, and he started to believe in his own ability and live up to the label he wore. He recently won a literary award for his short stories. Not all labels have this dramatic effect and some have a negative one. Below is the true story of Jeremy who found out during counselling that the labels which he had accepted as a child were still sticking to him, bringing pain and suffering.

CASE STUDY: JEREMY

At the age of thirty-two Jeremy took the brave step of going to a counsellor for help. He was an attractive young man with a good job and he had had a string of girlfriends, but his relationships had all ended in disaster. He was longing to get married and have a family of his own but he had begun to doubt that this could ever happen to him.

The counsellor explored carefully how he felt about the girls he went out with. 'I really loved Sue and I longed to tell her how I felt but I never quite managed it. I couldn't imagine somebody wanting me as a partner,' he said, 'and so whenever they said nice things to me I always felt they were just being kind. I never really believed them...' The counsellor continued to explore why it was that Jeremy lacked the confidence to express and to receive love. Jeremy told her what he had never told anyone else. He felt ugly. He felt that no one could ever really care for him because he was so unattractive. Eventually, they both discovered an early memory of his that made sense of his present feelings. At the age of five he had overheard a conversation that put a label on him for life. His mother was talking to her sister: 'When he was born I

was horrified. He was so ugly. He'll never be anything special, will he?' Jeremy froze. He could still remember the event years later.

GROUP ACTIVITY 1 (10 MINS)

DISCOVERING LABELS

Are any of the following labels stuck to you? Read through the list and jot down anything that relates, either past or present, to your own life. With another member of the group explore:

● **What the label means to you. Give your partner an example.**

● **Whether you can trace how this label came to be. Try and think of the first time you felt this about yourself.**

● **Are there any labels that you can identify which are not on this list? Add them.**

LABELS

☺ **I never get anything right.**
☺ **I am clumsy.**
☺ **I am lazy.**
☺ **I am fat.**
☺ **I am too big/small.**
☺ **I am always late.**
☺ **I am always a happy person.**
☺ **I am strong.**
☺ **I am weak.**
☺ **I am someone who looks after others.**
☺ **I am someone who needs looking after.**
☺ **I am a person who never trusts anybody.**
☺ **I am a victim.**
☺ **I am superior.**
☺ **I will never be any good.**

☺ **I am the life and soul of the party.**

☺ **I am frightened.**

☺ **I am beautiful.**

☺ **I am inferior.**

GROUP ACTIVITY 2 (15 MINS)

COUNSELLING JEREMY

● **Get into groups of two or three people. Your aim as a group is to help Jeremy on to the next step of self-awareness and personal growth.**

● **As a group explore the label of 'ugliness' that Jeremy received. What might this feel like to him? What other effects could it have had on him? How could it affect a person in her/his relationships? Work at the skill of empathy. See if you can increase your own sensitivity to somebody else's feelings:**

■ **What questions would you want to ask him?**

■ **Decide how you are going to go into this. What other areas of his life would you like to help him to explore? For example, is he successful at his work, does he make friends personally, does this sense of inferiority affect his whole life?**

For this exercise this is as far as it is useful to go. We shall be counselling fully later on in the book.

THE WORK OF J. B. ROTTER: THE LOCUS OF CONTROL

If you failed an examination what would be your first response? To blame yourself or to blame outside forces? If you got turned down for a job to what might you attribute the cause? To outside causes—the preference of the interviewers on the day—or to inside causes—your own performance at interview or the fact that you had not got the right background for the job?

The work of psychologist J. B. Rotter offers some very interesting ideas about how people attribute causes in their lives. He calls this attribution theory. This is a theory about how people learn to blame inside or outside forces for what happens to them. Rotter says that children attribute from a very early age. As they grow up they are learning to find a reason for the things that happen to them. All the time they are learning whether events are externally caused or whether it is themselves who are the cause of what happens to them.

Consider, for example, the parents who insist that their little boy should not cry. Their behaviour is almost always predictable. When the little boy cries his parents remove their affection temporarily. He very soon learns that he is relied upon not to cry. This enforces the idea of internal control: 'You must not cry. It's up to you not to let us down.' In contrast, imagine a little boy whose mother/father is either an alcoholic or subject for some reason to sudden mood swings. The parent is unpredictable. Very soon the little boy realizes that whatever behaviour he tries, it has little or no effect on how he is treated. He breaks a glass one day and is smacked and screamed at. The next day he spills the milk all over the table and his parents just laugh. That little boy has no internal control. For him, the events that happen are all caused by outside factors. J. B. Rotter says that children get fixed ideas that either they themselves are in control or that the outside world is the cause.

Think for a minute about what this means to the way a person functions and understands her/himself. If you have a high sense of internality then you, and only you, are to blame for the things that happen. Consistent behaviour becomes a very anxious event. The burden of self-achievement can even become unbearable. Many psychologists draw attention to the fact that, in middle-class child-rearing especially, the child is expected always to do well. 'You must win, you must pass,' is the label that gets stuck to her/him. Some families give tangible rewards for success at school or in examinations: a new bike, a hi-fi system, a computer and so on. That same family may give psychological punishment for failure: no rewards and no affection, or silence about the issue. One father actually got out his old school reports with a line of As and pointedly told his seven-year-old daughter: 'Why can't you do this? You're nothing like me when I was your age.'

Many children resort to learned helplessness. They learn to survive the tyranny of high expectations by becoming obviously helpless: ill, weak non-achievers, who are badly behaved and so forth. The strategy here is to self-adopt the label 'I am helpless' and then no one will expect anything different. Of course, not every child responds in this way. The world is full of adults who are still trying desperately to fulfil the highest expectations inherited from childhood, and who suffer overload, marital stress, ulcers and high levels of anxiety in their attempts to ward off the personal blame which will accrue if they fail. After all, you only have yourself to blame.

The following exercise helps you to identify your own tendencies to attribute cause. The ideas here are based on the Rotter Scale of Internal/External Control and with careful thought you will get an idea of your own habitual ways of responding. Unfortunately, we cannot reproduce the complete Rotter test because it has to be administered by people who are qualified to give psychometric tests to others.

PERSONAL REFLECTION/ SELF-EVALUATION

Individually, tick which of the following comments most concur with your point of view. Of course you will sometimes want to tick both or none at all but in order to have a go at the test you will have to register even a small preference.

1(a) Many of the unhappy things in people's lives are partly due to bad luck.

1(b) People's misfortunes result from the mistakes they make.

2(a) Without the right opportunities you cannot be an effective leader.

2(b) Capable people who fail to become leaders have not taken advantage of the opportunities given them.

3(a) This world runs because there are a few people who have maximum power, and there is not much that you or I can do about it.

3(b) An ordinary person in the street can have an influence in government decisions if s/he wants to.

4(a) Promotion is all about being in the right place at the right time.

4(b) Getting on in life depends on having the ability and determination to do it; luck has very little to do with it.

5(a) When all is said and done the bad things that happen to us are balanced by the good ones.

5(b) Most misfortunes are the result of ignorance, laziness or a lack of ability—maybe all three.

6(a) It's no good trying too hard to please people; if they like you, they like you and if they don't, they don't.

6(b) People are lonely because they don't make the effort to be friendly and meet other people.

If you got all (a)s you may have a high investment in fate: 'It all happens to me.' You tend to believe that external forces influence your life. It is easy to feel powerless and to inflict blame on others if this is your tendency.

If you got all (b)s you may have a high investment in internality: 'I have to be in control.' There are stresses if you think that you need to be so much in control. It is easy to feel a personal failure and to inflict blame on yourself.

If you got a fair mixture of (a)s and (b)s you are more balanced and more likely not to suffer the extremes of stress which locate themselves in having a narrow view of the world.

Be careful not to see this exercise as a reliable measure. It gives some indication of what you are like but you would need to have far more factors to test and evaluate in order to get a higher degree of accuracy.

Understanding how a person attributes cause can sometimes give you just the focus you need in the counselling situation. It might be that your client needs to rethink how her/his habitual patterns of locating cause can bring her/him problems. S/he may need to work hard at altering her/his own perceptions—unless of course s/he believes that childhood must always affect her/him and that s/he can never be changed. And then you have the difficult task of asking whether you can help her/him at all. For if nothing can change what hope is there for progress?

FOOD FOR THOUGHT

- Would addicted gamblers have a high external score in the locus of control test?

- Are there any links between the locus of control scores and your political vote?

- Would someone who believes strongly in predestination or has a strong dependence on God's guidance in her/his decision-making tend to have a high internal or external score? Or would it make no difference at all?

Personal Diary

LEARNING TO FORGIVE OTHERS AND YOURSELF

So far in this book we have looked at various insights and approaches from different psychologists and therapists. You may have warmed to some methods more than others. Now we are going to look at something which is distinctly Christian: the belief that forgiveness is a fundamental requirement for becoming a whole person, psychologically, spiritually and physically.

The focus of this unit is to look at the process of forgiveness and its possible effects on the well-being of anyone who gives or receives it. We look at the deep feelings of the individual who may well find it impossible to forgive. For example, relatives of people who have been abused or murdered often report that their own lives become more difficult. They suffer illness or accidents. You often hear someone say, 'Since this has happened it's ruined my life. I cannot forgive what this person has done to us.' Is this because bitterness, hatred and anger take energy and concentration away from our daily routine? Genuine forgiveness is something that heals.

✔ AIMS

The aims of this unit are:

- To examine some of the teaching of Jesus on the subject of forgiveness.

- To provide opportunities for you to think through how you set about forgiving yourself.

- To look at the levels of forgiveness required in human experience and to begin to see how a person could be helped towards the process.

- To provide you with models of others who have learned to forgive and their understanding of its benefits and effects.

STARTER ACTIVITY (10 MINS)

WHAT IS FORGIVENESS?

Is forgiveness a thing of the will—you decide to do it and then you bury the memories of what has been forgiven and that is the end of it? Or is forgiveness a gift from God—all we have to do is ask and receive it, and then it is ours?

Get into groups of two or three. One of you should record the main points of what is discussed. Discuss between yourselves the following points:

- What is forgiveness? Is it an act of will, a gift from God, an ongoing process in life which needs to be learned? Or is it a combination of all these and more? What does your group think?

- Discuss who you think is the most forgiving person you have ever encountered? What was s/he like? What were her/his personal attributes? What did s/he do? Is a forgiving nature something rare or something seen frequently in your community?

GROUP FEEDBACK

Each group has three minutes to feed back the main points of its discussion to the wider group.

JESUS' TEACHING ON THE POWER OF FORGIVENESS

In the gospel accounts, forgiveness is at the heart of the ministry and thinking of Jesus. There are many accounts which show different perspectives about the art, the process and the effects of forgiveness in a person's life. We will look at two stories in which Jesus shows forgiveness and, in the process, heals people's emotional and physical wounds.

STORY 1: JESUS AND THE WOMAN IN SIMON THE PHARISEE'S HOUSE (LUKE 7:36–50)

Now one of the Pharisees invited Jesus to have dinner with him, so he went to the Pharisee's house and reclined at the table. When a woman who had lived a sinful life in that town learned that Jesus was eating at the Pharisee's house, she brought an alabaster jar of perfume, and as she stood behind him at his feet weeping, she began to wet his feet with her tears. Then she wiped them with her hair, kissed them and poured perfume on them.

When the Pharisee who had invited him saw this, he said to himself: 'If this man were a prophet, he would know who is touching him and what kind of woman she is—that she is a sinner.'

Jesus answered him, 'Simon, I have something to tell you.'

'Tell me, teacher,' he said.

'Two men owed money to a certain money-lender. One owed him five hundred denarii, and the other fifty. Neither of them had the money to pay him back, so he cancelled the debts of both. Now which of them will love him more?

Simon replied, 'I suppose the one who had the bigger debt cancelled.'

'You have judged correctly,' Jesus said.

Then he turned towards the woman and said to Simon, 'Do you see this woman? I came into your house. You did not give me any water for my feet, but she wet my feet with her tears and wiped them with her hair. You did not give me a kiss, but this woman, from the time I entered has not stopped kissing my feet. You did not put oil on my head, but she has poured perfume on my feet. Therefore, I tell you, her many sins have been forgiven—for she loved much. But he who has been forgiven little loves little.'

Then Jesus said to her, 'Your sins are forgiven.'

The other guests began to say among themselves, 'Who is this who even forgives sins?'

Jesus said to the woman, 'Your faith has saved you; go in peace.'

Here Jesus says that the person who forgives the most is loved the most and that the person who is forgiven more can love more.

GROUP ACTIVITY 1 (15–20 MINS)

This exercise is designed for you to develop empathy, and to use your own feelings and creativity in using the Bible. There needs to be quiet in the group.

1. Your leader reads the story of Jesus at the house of Simon the Pharisee (Luke 7:36–50) above.

2. One person then reads the following commentary out loud to the whole group. It is background material for the exercise.

COMMENTARY

THE PHARISEE

Simon is a Pharisee. It is his house. The Pharisees wielded religious power. They were ordinary men, not priests, who kept the religious law, but some of them added to it so that it became difficult to keep. For instance, the law of Moses said to keep the Sabbath as a day of rest but the Pharisees went to such extremes that even cutting your toenails was counted as work. Many Pharisees were genuine men of faith but looked down on common people as 'sinners'. They despised the woman in this story because no respectable woman would enter this place on her own or touch a man who was not her husband. She could only have been a sinful woman and she would have made Jesus 'unclean'.

What would Simon have been feeling:

● When he saw the woman's actions?

● When he heard Jesus' reply to himself?

THE WOMAN

We know little about her except that she had brought expensive oil with her to rub on Jesus' feet. It was the custom in the hot Middle East that after a guest had travelled to your house in the dust, you would have water available for feet to be washed and refreshed. Jesus had received no such treatment. Instead this woman, risking ridicule and contempt from the Pharisees and perhaps risking rejection from Jesus, approached Jesus with her offering.

What emotions:

● Would have prompted such an action from her?

● Did she feel when she entered the house?

● Resulted from Jesus' acceptance of her despite all the religious views of those present?

THE DISCIPLES

Jesus' twelve disciples were with him on most of his journeys and visits. Sometimes all of them accompanied him, sometimes just Peter, James and John. This story in Luke does not mention that the disciples were present

but it is likely that some of them were. If they were, what might they have been feeling when they saw the intimacy of this woman?

JESUS

In his gospel, Luke does not tell us how Jesus felt about this offering but he does tell us what Jesus said to Simon, to those gathered and to the woman. What emotions do you think this whole event may have evoked for Jesus?

THE OTHERS IN THE GATHERING

Who else might have been there? How might they have felt?

---

3. Now choose one of these characters to identify with. Elect one member of the group to read the story again but this time slowly, stopping to pause for a moment at appropriate points. Instead of just reading the story, participate in it by closing your eyes and visualizing the scene from the perspective of your character. Remember to stick to the story. You cannot introduce new events or put extra words into anybody's mouth but you can bring the story alive by imagining the feelings and emotions that generated this event. When the story is finished stay quiet for a minute or two. When you feel ready, 'return' to the reality of the group.

4. If you like, share the experience you had in doing this exercise with a friend. Alternatively, write up your own feelings and thoughts in a spiritual diary. Diaries of this sort can be very helpful in marking your own spiritual pilgrimage from day to day.

THE POWER OF FORGIVENESS

The power of forgiveness in the counselling situation is as real today as it was in the time of Jesus.

CASE-STUDY: SARA AND THE POWER OF HER FORGIVENESS

Sara was twenty-seven years old and she was married to Andy, a successful businessman and a very loving husband. They were both committed Christians. Andy and Sara came for counselling together to Chris who was a trainee counsellor and also a committed Christian. Ever since the time they had married everything seemed to have gone wrong. At the time of their wedding Sara's jaw had locked. This made eating, kissing and expressing herself a very frustrating process. But there were other problems, too. Sara felt bad about herself. She felt that she was inadequate, unattractive and that Andy had had a rough time marrying her in this condition. Various medics had given advice but the jaw was still locked. Sara told Chris that although she could not change the state of her jaw she hoped to find a solution to her ever-decreasing self-esteem before she slipped into the depression that she most feared.

After an introductory session, Chris decided to start asking questions about the wedding day on which the jaw got locked. 'Tell me about the events surrounding your marriage,' he said. 'It was very difficult,' said Sara, 'you see, my mother really spoilt the whole event for both of us.' Andy showed empathy and put his hand on her shoulder. 'I've always tried to please my mother and I love her very much but something happened the day I married which will stay with me for ever. I was getting dressed in my lovely white gown and mother was helping me. She had never been fond of Andy, but I thought that when I married him she would grow to love him as much as I did. Anyway, I remember looking at my reflection in the mirror and feeling so happy when all of

a sudden I caught a glimpse of my mother behind me. The mirror showed me the look on her face: it showed hate and rejection and spite and then she said: "You can never have both him and me—after today, you and I are parting company." I froze. That's all I remember, the shock of it. I longed to say something but the words wouldn't come out and within hours my jaw was locked.'

After hearing this Chris suggested that they try something together. 'I don't know that I'm on the right track,' he said, 'but I get the feeling that we should start with forgiveness. Would you be willing to start the process of forgiving your mother for this. It may take time but I think it's worth exploring together.' Sara said she was willing to try. Chris began to finish the session with a short time of prayer in which he invited Sara to voice the hurt and pain of this event to God, and to ask for his help in learning to forgive her mother.

The prayer had hardly finished when Chris, Andy and Sara heard a clacking and a knocking sound. Sara's jaw was moving around in jerks and with clicking sounds. Within a few minutes the locked jaw was free.

Chris had counselled many other people during the course of his training but he had never seen anything like this. Even now, he rarely sees anything so dramatic but he has learned first hand the power of the forgiveness process. Even if there are no visible effects he observes how forgiving others can release emotions and pain, and help to set people free from the negative power of their darkest memories.

STORY 2: THE HEALING OF THE PARALYTIC (MARK 2:1–12 AND PARALLEL PASSAGES)

A few days later, when Jesus again entered Capernaum, the people heard that he had come home. So many gathered that there was no room left, not even outside the door, and he preached the word to them. Some men came, bringing to him a paralytic, carried by four of them. Since they could not get him to Jesus because of the crowd, they made an opening in the roof above Jesus and, after digging through it, lowered the mat the paralysed man was lying on. When Jesus saw their faith, he said to the paralytic, 'Son, your sins are forgiven.'

Now some teachers of the law were sitting there, thinking to themselves, 'Why does this fellow talk like that? He's blaspheming! Who can forgive sins but God alone?'

Immediately Jesus knew in his spirit that this was what they were thinking in their hearts, and he said to them, 'Why are you saying these things? Which is easier: to say to the paralytic, 'Your sins are forgiven,' or to say, 'Get up, take your mat and walk'? But that you may know that the Son of Man has authority on earth to forgive sins....' He said to the paralytic, 'I tell you, get up, take your mat and go home.' He got up, took his mat and walked out in full view of them all. This amazed everyone and they praised God, saying, 'We have never seen anything like this!'

Here Jesus links this man's physical healing with his need for forgiveness. Look at the process involved in this story:

- Who does what ?

- What attitudes can be seen in this story?

- How do you think forgiveness worked in this situation?

FORGIVENESS AND PHYSICAL HEALTH

In the healing of the paralytic Jesus identifies the relationship between the man's inner need for forgiveness and his physical state. Sometimes people come for help because their health is weak and they feel that other aspects of their lives are weak, too. An increasing number of professionals involved in health care are now taking a holistic approach to medicine. They feel that there is more to

health than just physical well-being, and that the mental, emotional and spiritual aspects of people's lives all influence how healthy we are. Occasionally, this is dramatically visible and at other times it is indiscernible. The case study of Sara is an unusual one but it is a true story, although her name has been changed to guard her privacy.

GROUP ACTIVITY 2 (10 MINS)

SKILLS OF FORGIVENESS

As a whole group listen to what a few people have said as they have tried to practise the art of forgiveness in response to specific situations and then discuss the questions below.

A DRINK-DRIVING ACCIDENT

A six-year-old is killed by a man driving fast and dangerously who has drunk too much because of depression. The parents, a Church of England minister and his wife, are committed Christians. They think of this in the light of Christ's teachings. The father responds:

The reason I can forgive my son's killing is that I know something of where that man comes from... I didn't feel so distant from him that I couldn't understand him.

When we bottle up anger we destroy ourselves by the failure to forgive.

I felt I had to forgive—I couldn't forgive myself if I didn't. I knew I couldn't receive God's forgiveness unless I could forgive others.

We have to find a way of hating sin and not hating the sinner.

Forgiveness is not an optional extra—we have to do it.

A HIJACK

Catherine does not declare any religious convictions. She was involved in the Karachi hijack in which 120 people were killed or maimed. Her own body was damaged, leaving her leg and pelvis shattered. Her perceptions of the forgiving process are deep, penetrating and reflective.

To forgive you have to be actively involved. It's something you do. When I walk I sweat. It takes such energy that I don't have any to give to forgiveness.

In order to be healthy I have to accept what has happened, then move on to live. But to take a step towards them (the terrorists)—I will never do that, because they don't deserve it. They chose to kill and maim 120 people. They planned it.

I'm not vindictive even now. But if you have an implacable other part, for example the terrorist, they will do it again. How do you forgive if there's no relationship?

Interviewer: *Can you forgive?*

Catherine: *The intention is there but I don't know if I can cross that bridge. If a terrorist came and stood in front of me and said 'I'm sorry', then maybe I could begin. But how can you cross a bridge that doesn't exist?*

FAMILY BETRAYAL

Colin Caffell's mother- and father-in-law, two sons and his wife Sheila were shot and killed by his brother-in-law, Jeremy (Sheila's brother). Jeremy tried to make it look as though Sheila had killed them, but was later arrested. The story made national news. The motive was money. Here are some of the things that Colin said when interviewed:

I have given up any claim I have for revenge.

Forgiveness is inner—a personal thing rather than something that one has to be seen to be doing.

Forgiveness is where I'm at for myself.

Interviewer: *How could you think of forgiving someone who did this. Do you not feel disloyal to them?*

Colin: *No. If I allow myself to be involved in hate, rage, bitterness I am letting them down in that way.*

Interviewer: *The motive was money—do you not find that harder to forgive?*

Colin: *Yes—but what made Jeremy so hateful of his family—what happened to that child in him?*

GROUP DISCUSSION

- **Where does forgiveness happen: in the head, the stomach, the pores of body, where?**

- **Does it have to be a two-way process? What happens if the wrongdoers do not admit to guilt or do not care about forgiveness? Can we forgive them for not caring?**

- **Is forgiveness a one-off event or is it a continual process to be practised day in-day out?**

- **Do you have to do anything with forgiveness? Do you have to act upon it?**

PERSONAL REFLECTION

Individually, think about any individual in your own life who has hurt you or caused you pain. Now focus and meditate upon the questions below. You may wish to record your thoughts in your personal diary or talk to someone in the counselling role who can help you process things further.

- **How far have you gone towards forgiving her/him?**

- **What needs yet to be done?**

- **Who can help you to think further about it?**

- **How do you know when forgiveness has taken place?**

- **Can you test it? For instance, can you write or phone somebody whom you** have cut out of your life because s/he has done something unforgivable?

● If the person who upset you was sitting in front of you at this moment in time, what would your reactions be? Would you be tense, would you have to exert energy to control your feelings? Or would you feel you had some measure of love for her/him although you did not want to be friends or have regular contact?

These are hard questions but important to test if we are to access understanding of whether we can forgive or not.

One final question: once you have learned forgiveness does it become easier to do again?

FOOD FOR THOUGHT

Here are some quotations for you to think about (taken from Wesley Carr, *The Pastor as Theologian*, 1989):

A major problem with people who feel acute guilt is that they cannot accept themselves. It is no use speaking to them of the accepting grace of God, since they have insufficient sense of their self to which to apply it. The pastor needs the model of the atonement to work with rather than any easy assumption about its benefits.

The pastor is involved in counselling. His role is to embody this acceptance by God and willingly receive projections on behalf of God before attempting to offer them back in interpretation so that people have space to discover how they can accept themselves... this is a different emphasis to that of the traditional priest who has set rules and ritual, for example confession and absolution.

Forgiveness is not a feeling or a state but an experience that is demonstrated in action.

Forgiveness of the past implies future action based upon that past. So any notion of

eradicating that past is theologically, pastorally and psychologically false.

Here are some quotations from the New Testament on the theme of forgiveness:

Forgive us our debts, as we also have forgiven our debtors.
Matthew 6:12; see Luke 11:4

For if you forgive men when they sin against you, your heavenly Father will also forgive you. But if you do not forgive men their sins, your Father will not forgive your sins.
Matthew 6:14–15

'But so that you may know that the Son of Man has authority on earth to forgive sins...' Then he said to the paralytic, 'Get up, take your mat and go home.'
Matthew 9:6; see Mark 2:10, Luke 5:24

Then Peter came to Jesus and asked, 'Lord, how many times shall I forgive my brother when he sins against me? Up to seven times?'
Matthew 18:21

'This is how my heavenly Father will treat each of you unless you forgive your brother from your heart.'
Matthew 18:35

'Why does this fellow talk like that? He's blaspheming! Who can forgive sins but God alone?'
Mark 2:7; see Luke 5:21

'And when you stand praying, forgive, if you hold anything against anyone, forgive him, so that your Father in heaven may forgive you your sins.'
Mark 11:25

'Do not judge, and you will not be judged. Do not condemn, and you will not be condemned. Forgive, and you will be forgiven.'
Luke 6:37

'So watch yourselves; if your brother sins, rebuke him, and if he repents, forgive him. If he sins against you seven times in a day, and seven times comes back to you and says, "I repent," forgive him.'
Luke 17:3–4

Jesus said, 'Father, forgive them; for they do not know what they are doing.' And they divided up his clothes by casting lots.
Luke 23:34

'If you forgive anyone his sins, they are forgiven; if you do not forgive them, they are not forgiven.'
John 20:23

Now instead, you ought to forgive and comfort him, so that he will not be overwhelmed by excessive sorrow.
2 Corinthians 2:7

If you forgive anyone, I also forgive him. And what I have forgiven—if there was anything to forgive—I have forgiven in the sight of Christ for your sake…'
2 Corinthians 2:10

Bear with each other and forgive whatever grievances you may have against one another. Forgive as the Lord forgave you.
Colossians 3:13

If we confess our sins, he is faithful and just and will forgive our sins and purify us from all unrighteousness.
1 John 1:9

SELF-EVALUATION

Individually, and in private, complete as many of the following sentences as you can in order to evaluate your own thinking and responses to forgiveness:

● **I think that forgiveness is when ......**
....

● **I have received forgiveness from**
.... **when ....**
....

● **I have learned to forgive and it means that I have to ....**

● **I have a lot to learn about forgiving others, especially ....**

● **There is one thing I just cannot forgive and that is ....**

● **There is one thing I cannot be forgiven for and that is ....**
....

Now think about what you would like to change and how you might go about this. You may wish to talk this over with a good friend.

Personal Diary

3.3 LISTENING AND PARAPHRASING
TWO WAYS OF SHOWING CARE

The process of listening and attending to someone else is not an easy matter. Think how often you have been spoken to when your mind was suddenly elsewhere. The other person might even have been saying something important but you were oblivious to it because you had mentally just 'gone shopping for food', 'rehearsed your excuses for being late' or 'thought about what you had to do next'.

Research done on listening and attending behaviour shows the difficulty of concentrating on two complex verbal tasks at the same time. For example, if you are rehearsing what you want to say next, then it is very difficult to attend to what the other person is saying. You may be burning to say something yourself and even interrupt the other speaker before s/he is finished.

It is obvious that to be an effective helper you have to pay attention to what the other person is saying. It is just as important that the person you are helping should feel that s/he is being attended to. The knowledge that they are being listened to with accuracy can be a healing source in itself to many people. It shows them that they are valued, that they are worth listening to. This unit is therefore a very important one for anyone wishing to counsel or help another person.

✔ AIMS

Our aims in this unit are:

- To help you to identify and gain effectiveness in a range of listening skills.

- To practise and use the skill of accurately paraphrasing what someone has said.

- To begin to counsel and be counselled yourself.

- To help you to evaluate your own strengths and weaknesses in listening and attending to other people.

STARTER ACTIVITY (10 MINS)

YOUR LISTENING SELF

This is an exercise to help you to evaluate your own listening skills. In some conversations listening is not so important. For example, you might be admiring a garden together and there may be a natural flow of praise for the beauty of the place. In this situation you would not be using all your listening skills, that is, the art of asking open questions or paraphrasing what has just been said about the flowers. But in the counselling situation even the smallest throw-away comment can be a clue to the real issues at stake. When it is important, are you a good listener?

- Look at the list on page 77. Which of these statements come closest to how you habitually behave when listening to someone else? You may wish to add to the list.

- When you have done this, join with someone else and choose to talk about something you find easy and something you find difficult about listening to others.

- When someone else is telling you about her/his own experiences for a considerable length of time, do you tend to:

  - Switch off?

  - Get distracted and think of important things that need saying or doing?

  - Tend to be interested in all s/he has to say?

  - Filter what is interesting and think your own thoughts for the rest of the time?

  - Rehearse what you are going to say as soon as s/he has finished?

  - Interrupt her/him so that you do not have to listen for too long?

  - Try to find something in your own experience which fits in with her/his?

  - Think of questions you can ask her/him in order to show interest?

  - Try to remember what has been said?

  - Something else?

COUNSELLING SKILL 1: MINIMUM ENCOURAGEMENT AND SILENCE

It is well known that new counsellors often respond too quickly to what someone has said—sometimes before the other person has completely finished what it was s/he wanted to say. This can lead clients into thinking that they have not really been listened to because the counsellor was more interested in what s/he her/himself had to say.

Ivey and Authier in *Microcounselling* (2nd edition, 1978) give evidence that the use of a minimum of encouragement by the counsellor led to longer periods of talking from the client. In addition to this, if the counsellor always waited a full five seconds before responding then the client initiated more discussion in 25 per cent of instances.

Minimum encouragement can be given in several different ways but it always means just what it says: that the counsellor's response is minimal. This can be very important in the early stages of counselling someone because you need to gain accurate information from her/him, and also to give her/him the assurance that s/he is someone who is valued and treated with respect. Minimum encouragement can take the form of:

- head nodding;

- smiling;

- sounds and comments, for example: 'Yes,' 'Do repeat that again,' 'Please do go on';

- repeating a word or two from the last phrase.

Here is an example of using the last word or two from the last phrase:

Client: It's just that she was always criticizing me when I was a child.

Counsellor: Criticizing you?

Client: Yes, you know the sort of thing. 'Mary, you should know better,' and 'Mary, nobody will ever love you if you behave like that.' I used to sit on my own and think how I could avoid this criticism.

Counsellor: Avoid it?

Client: Yes, and I did avoid it. I used to make sure I was always ill or sick especially when she looked like she was going to go off the deep end at me, and then my father would rescue me.

Counsellor: He would rescue you?

Client: He always rescued me by putting himself between mother and myself. I guess that's why I'm so disappointed with my husband—he won't rescue me, he expects me to sort things out.
Counsellor: I think we're getting somewhere. Tell me about your husband.

GROUP ACTIVITY 1 (10–15 MINS)

This activity is the first of many where real counselling begins. This is not a role-play and you are asked to choose any of the following themes to talk about which are real issues for you. If there is nothing suitable on the list then consider what you can comfortably choose to speak about with someone else:

THEMES

- Anxiety about the future.

- Lack of self-confidence.

- Managing personal anger and frustration.

- A current difficult issue.

To start the activity:

- Agree to work with someone else in pairs and label yourselves A and B. A is the counsellor; B is the client.

- From the start both A and B are to be professional. A will monitor the seating arrangements, then start off the counselling process by inviting B to share her/his concerns. B will bring a real concern for counselling. A must stick to the rule *not to advise, offer solutions or even make comments on the issues.* This exercise is to practise a particular skill, the skill of minimum encouragement. It is done on the understanding that confidentiality must be maintained outside of this situation.

- This is a ten- to fifteen-minute exercise depending on the time available. It is important not to change roles here because we are going to exchange places (that is, A takes on B's part) in the next exercise.

- At completion, both A and B discuss what the experience was like for them. How did it feel to counsel and be counselled? What did you learn? Was it difficult and if so why? What did the other person look like? If you did it again what would you like to change?

COUNSELLING SKILL 2: USING QUESTIONS IN THE HELPING PROCESS

Questions can either help or hinder the counselling process. If the counsellor fires a long series of questions at the client it can be seen as more of an interrogation than a helpful conversation. However, questions do have to be asked in order to gain information and explore various issues—especially with a person who does not find it easy to talk about her/himself.

It is very useful to look at the sort of questions a counsellor can ask. Here we explore two types of question: closed and open.

CLOSED QUESTIONS

A closed question tends to invite a yes/no answer or it may just gain you factual information. Here are some closed questions:

- 'Are you feeling sad?'

- 'Did you say anything after that?'

- 'Who did you go to for help?'

- 'When did this happen?'

Closed questions may be needed at certain times. However, a consecutive series of closed questions results in the counsellor talking more than the client.

OPEN QUESTIONS

Open questions often begin with the words 'why', 'how', 'might', 'what' or 'could'.

- **'Why' questions** tend to produce motives, explanations and reasons.

- **'How' questions** tend to bring about feelings and processes.

- **'Might' questions** help to explore future options.

- **'What' questions** produce facts and information.

- **'Could' or 'Would' questions** ask the client to explore her/his potential.

Fritz Perls, who we have already mentioned (Unit 1.2) in connection with Gestalt therapy, makes an interesting point about 'why' questions. He says that 'why' questions can be embarrassing because some people are not aware of the actual motives and reasons for their behaviour. When they fail to answer or stumble over their reply it can have an effect on how they feel they are being perceived by the counsellor. This is not to say that 'why' questions cannot be used, but they must be considered in context. They can block the other person from saying much more.

GROUP ACTIVITY 2 (10–15 MINS)

USING QUESTIONS

- **Continue in the same pairs as were formed for group counselling activity 1. Exchange roles; if you were the counsellor, play the role of the client and if you were the client, take the role of counsellor. As in the previous exercise, label yourselves A and B, with A as the counsellor and B as the client.**

- **B selects a real issue and A begins by asking her/him to talk about it.**

- **A is going to use the following two skills throughout the conversation:**

  - **minimal encouragement; and**

  - **formulating open questions.**

  This should mean that there is no actual conversation going on; B alone should be expressing her/himself and this should be punctuated by encouragement and key questions.

  The activity lasts between ten and fifteen minutes, after which A and B talk in a different capacity about what the experience was like for them.

COUNSELLING SKILL 3: REFLECTING THE CONTENT OF CONVERSATIONS BY PARAPHRASING

How does somebody know that you have understood and empathized with her/his situation? One way of doing this is to develop the ability to feed back to the other person the main content of what s/he has been saying, that is, paraphrasing. You may remember that Carl Rogers believes that this is one of the major components of the client's feeling of being valued. For Rogers it is a central part of the counselling process because the art of paraphrasing is one way of responding to the other person without judging or evaluating what s/he has said. It can be very powerful indeed.

When you begin to practise the art of paraphrasing it is important to avoid merely repeating someone's words in parrot fashion. This can be taken to mean that you are insincere. It is worth showing what this kind of repetition sounds like:

Client: *I am such a failure. Everything I do goes wrong. I have tried and tried to please my boss but I never get anything right.*

Counsellor: You feel your life is a failure, everything you do goes wrong and that you have tried to please your boss but you never get anything right.

The aim in skilful paraphrasing is for the client to see that you, the counsellor, have both heard and understood what has been said:

Client: I have never found it easy to make friends. In fact I've quite enjoyed being on my own, but recently it's meant I have no one to turn to when things are so hard and I dread going home from work to the silence of an empty house.

Counsellor: So you used to enjoy your privacy but now you are realizing that relationships are important to you at this time in your life and you need more than an empty house to come home to.

Client: I can't cope any longer. My husband hardly ever comes home before midnight and the kids are uncontrollable. I feel a failure as a wife and a mother.

Counsellor: Your husband's absence and the pressure from the kids is causing you to seriously doubt your ability to look after your family.

Accurate paraphrasing is a great asset to the counselling process. It helps the counsellor to arrive at a better understanding of the client's experience and the way s/he sees the world. Nevertheless, as we have already mentioned in a previous chapter, people often have their own private ways of understanding different words and phrases, and the counsellor should make sure that the meaning of what is said is shared.

If there is not a close exchange of meaning it can lead to distortion. If the counsellor does not get the phrase or sentence quite right, it can confuse the client. S/he could go off in different directions of conversation or s/he may even accept the counsellor's distortion as an accurate reflection of her own experience. It is very useful to look for non-verbal cues,

for example a hesitancy in the voice or a querying look in the eyes, which say that something has gone wrong. To comment on this sort of information involves a degree of interpretation on the part of the counsellor. This is best checked out with the client as practically as possible. For example:

Counsellor: I have noticed that whenever you talk about your sister your eyes look downwards and there is a tension in your face. What do you think? What does this mean to you?

The client may then be encouraged to talk about issues concerning her/his sister or alternatively the client may deny the interpretation that has been made. When the latter happens there is little point in pressing the matter further. It may or may not have been a misperception on your part. Sometimes, however, you may be anticipating feelings which the client may be willing to deal with in a later session.

Distortion is a difficult problem to deal with and it is important to create the sort of client-counsellor relationship that permits the client to correct you if you have misunderstood. It is easy to pretend that you have understood what the other person is saying. This should be resisted. It is much easier and confusion is avoided if you are honest:

Counsellor: I'm sorry, I haven't quite understood and I want to get it right. Tell me again about…

This kind of statement not only clears the meaning between you, but it can also contribute a great deal to enhancing the relationship because it shows that accuracy counts with you and that what the person says is important to you.

One note of caution. Once the skill of reflecting content has been learned it can become a mechanical affair if you are not careful. When counsellors get together for conferences it is not unknown to hear people chatting and doing nothing but reflecting content. Once this becomes obvious it can be very annoying. Sidney Jourard in his book *The Transparent Self* (1971), tells the following story:

I was never in therapy with a 'Rogerian' [somebody who uses the methods of Carl Rogers] but one of my colleagues lived this approach. She and I did part-time vocational counselling… One day I went to work feeling terribly depressed. I said to my then colleague, 'Oh, Gloria, I don't know if I can face today. I feel rotten.' Gloria, a PhD, turned to me. Up to that point, it had been 'Sid' and 'Gloria'. But as soon as I uttered my despair and depression, a glaze came over her eyes. I felt myself transmuted from 'Sid' into a 'client'. Her face assumed an expression that was supposed to be warmth, and then she said, 'You feel pretty rotten, don't you Sid?' That ended the dialogue as far as I was concerned.

Some days we all feel down and slightly depressed but it doesn't mean we need counselling—we may need more sleep!

GROUP ACTIVITY 3 (10–15 MINS)

● Get into pairs and indicate who is A and who is B. A is to counsel and B is to be the client. Again the issues discussed will be real ones and the situation will be a short time of real counselling. This is not role-play.

● Look at the subjects below and either choose one which relates to your own situation or suggest a topic of your own. You have ten minutes in which to talk.

● A, the counsellor, has only one task during this session and that is to reflect back from time to time on what has been said, using the paraphrasing techniques mentioned above.

THEMES

☺ Getting older and showing your age.

☺ Problems with money.

☺ Lack of promotion/progress in work situation.

☺ Coping with demands.

☺ A current difficult issue.

GROUP FEEDBACK

When the time is up everyone groups together for a different purpose to discuss what that was like for both the counsellor and the client. How hard was it? Did anyone begin to feel it was a useful skill? What did it achieve?

CHECKLIST FOR LISTENING

☺ Listen with attention, without interrupting.

☺ Remember what has been said to you.

☺ Listen for the cues which are not obvious but which you can feel happening.

☺ Watch for the non-verbal clues which help you to understand feelings.

☺ Practise tolerating pauses and small periods of silence. Resist the temptation to break silence.

☺ Practise as far as you can the skill of empathy, that is, entering the life-world of the other person.

☺ Promote an atmosphere of comfort and relaxed interaction with each other.

CHECKLIST FOR RESPONDING

☺ Use minimal encouragement: 'yes', 'mm', 'please continue' or the last few words of what your client has said.

☺ Keep questions to a minimum unless you need information or you want to open up discussion of something in detail, in which case use open-ended questions.

☺ If you don't quite understand, say so.

☺ Paraphrase or reflect accurately as a way of prompting the client, as a sign that you are listening or as a way of finding out whether you have heard correctly.

☺ Avoid being judgmental.

☺ Avoid speaking too often, too soon or too much.

SELF-EVALUATION

Look at the checklists above and give yourself a grade out of 5 for each skill listed:

Score 5 for *extremely proficient.*

Score 4 for *proficient.*

Score 3 for *all right but could improve.*

Score 2 for *weak.*

Score 1 for *I need to learn this skill, it is not in my repertoire.*

Now spend some time thinking about how you can set about improving these counselling and communication skills in your everyday life.

Practise the art of minimum encouragement in your wider friendships and family. Decide that you will deliberately leave short periods of silence after someone has spoken or consciously attend to her/him carefully without interrupting. Evaluate whether this has any effect on the way you communicate with each other.

PERSONAL REFLECTION

Think for a minute about the people with whom you come into daily contact: neighbours, friends at work, your partner, son/daughter, social worker. Who do you find it hard to listen to? Why? What sort of things help one person to listen to another? Choose someone who you find it difficult to listen to and make a plan about how you could improve your listening skills.

Personal Diary

Module 4

LEARNING TO IDENTIFY AND EXPRESS FEELINGS

4.1 REFLECTING FEELINGS
THE ART OF IDENTIFYING FEELINGS

How do you feel at the moment? Comfortable, tired, anxious, expectant or fulfilled? At any given moment in time and situation a range of feelings is present within us. Yet for many people feelings are not easy to identify—we tend to experience them rather than to verbalize them in the course of everyday life.

Feelings play an important part in the problems that are presented to you when you counsel someone. Think of some of the feelings that people bring to counselling: apathy, grief, indecision, loneliness, anger, confusion, frustration, inadequacy. These are just a few emotions for which people have to find coping strategies.

In Unit 3.3 we focused on reflecting the content of what someone else says. In this unit we look at reflecting the feelings of that person. It is not always easy to distinguish feelings from content but the skilled helper is able to reflect both simultaneously. At times it may be useful for counsellors to focus entirely on feelings. This is useful in the case of individuals who over-intellectualize their problems.

✔ AIMS

The aims of this unit are:

- To provide you with opportunities to increase your own self-awareness by identifying your own feelings in present experience.

- To explore the skill of putting feelings into words.

- To provide you with different models or ways of reflecting feeling in the counselling process.

- To define the process of empathy and to develop your own ability to empathize with those you counsel.

STARTER ACTIVITY

LOCATING FEELINGS
What are your feelings at the moment? This activity helps the whole group or the individual working on her/his own to explore feelings with metaphors.

- **Someone is elected to be group leader and to use the following script to oversee the activity.**

- **The leader asks the group to answer the following types of questions. Answers should be volunteered to the whole group:**

  - **Today/tonight if your feelings were to be described as a colour, what colour would they be?**

  - **What shade of that colour?**

  - **Why did you choose that colour?**

The following responses from one group show different levels of awareness:

Pam: I am green, a rich, deep shade of green tonight because I feel reflective and in tune with everybody in the group.

Ivor: I am a pale misty colour of grey because I feel as if life is all but clear. In fact, I think the grey represents a kind of fog. It's not life-threatening but it just confuses where things are in my life.

Myra: I am red, a bright flaming red, because I am furious about what has been happening to me at work.

REFLECTING FEELINGS

There are many ways in which a counsellor can reflect the feelings which s/he perceives in the counselling situation. The following gives minimal steps for the counsellor to use:

- **The feeling must be labelled.** This might be by repeating and using the actual words used by the client, or by offering observations of non-verbal signals.

- **Helpful sentence introductions can be:** 'You seem to feel…', 'It sounds like you feel…', or 'I sense that you're feeling as though…' (add the emotion which is being labelled).

- Certain phrases may be used for **additional clarification and maximum accuracy,** for example: 'You seem to feel… when… happens or when you talk about…'.

- **Reflection on feelings needs to be done in the here and now,** in present experience, that is, at or close to the time that the client is talking about them. This way the feelings can be discussed as they are experienced, not when they have passed and connection with them may be distant.

EXAMPLES OF DIFFERENT WAYS TO REFLECT FEELINGS

There are no right and wrong ways of reflecting feelings, but the following examples will help you to get some indication of the process itself:

Client: I would like some advice about changing my job soon… it's getting on top of me… though whatever I do, I'll probably never be any good at it.

Counsellor: I think you are saying that you feel dissatisfied and overwhelmed with what you are doing, and at the same time that you feel unable to cope with any job.

Client: It has taken me a long time to come for help, and I would never have come if it wasn't absolutely essential. But I feel very awkward and tense just sitting here now.

Counsellor: You feel desperate for help or you wouldn't have come. But facing me at this moment you feel nervous and closed up.

Client: I have been going out with him for nearly two years now but he continually upsets me by refusing to even consider marrying me although he wants us both to stay together. I wish I could make up my mind whether to finish the relationship or just stay with him in the hope of things working out.

Counsellor: What I hear you saying is that you feel hurt and rejected by his refusal, and you also feel upset by your own indecision.

Sometimes the feelings expressed in the client's words are different from those that are being expressed non-verbally. This may be an instance when the counsellor chooses to confront the client with the discrepancy.

GROUP ACTIVITY 1 (20 MINS)

OBSERVING AND IDENTIFYING FEELINGS

This activity is designed to give you the opportunity to consolidate what you have learned so far from this training course. It also gives you the chance to sharpen your observation and to practise the important skill of being able to reflect back accurately the feeling states that people go through in counselling.

- Get into groups of three (or four) people. Label yourselves A, B, C (and D). A is the counsellor; B is the client; and C/D are observers. Both observers should have a notepad and pencil. Seat yourselves so that A and B are comfortable, and so that the observers can see everything but are not obtrusive.

- Below is a short list of themes for this counselling session. B chooses anything from this list which is real for her/him or s/he can add any other topic of concern. Once again, this exercise is at its best when the issues are real and living rather than being role-play.

THEMES

🙂 Personal inadequacy.

🙂 A personal relationship in difficulty.

🙂 Coping with loss or bereavement.

🙂 Another issue of your own choosing.

The aim of this exercise is for B to explore her/his own issues, and for A to use all the listening and responding skills s/he has so far practised. In addition, s/he should make sure that s/he attempts to identify feelings present in this session.

The role of C and D, the observers, is to concentrate on what is actually happening during the counselling session. Make notes and comments on the categories of behaviour in the following checklist and be prepared to feed back to your group what you observed at the end.

CHECKLIST

- Eye contact between counsellor and client

- Movement and gestures

- Silence

- Posture

- Feelings identified?

- Open questions asked

- Closed questions asked

- Did either counsellor or client become uncomfortable. What happened?

- Anything else?

Now reassemble in your groups. Help each other to feed back on what the session was like. Counsellor first: *How did you feel things went?* Then the client: *Were you helped in any way to focus on things?* The observers then read out the notes they took and discuss them with the others: *What struck you the most?*

THE RANGE OF FEELINGS: EXPANDING YOUR LANGUAGE

An obvious, but not infallible, way of finding out what people feel is to listen to their **feeling words and phrases**. Picking up feeling words and phrases is rather like rewording something, but your focus is on the emotion, not the pure information or content, of what is said. You may even cause offence if you have to ask someone how s/he feels when s/he has actually just told you in feeling words and phrases. Feeling expressions can be colloquial: for example, 'I'm down', 'under the weather' or 'on top of the world'. It is worth noting that it is not necessary when reflecting feeling to always put 'You feel' before stating the emotion. Sometimes 'You're' is sufficient: for example, 'You're frustrated' instead of, 'You feel frustrated.' The box on page 89 contains a list of feeling words.

Feeling words

accepted	doomed	optimistic	uneasy
affectionate	ecstatic	powerful	unloved
aggressive	energetic	pain	unsupported
ambitious	envious	peaceful	unwanted
angry	frightened	pressured	vulnerable
anxious	faint-hearted	protected	violent
apathetic	grieving	rejected	wanted
appreciated	guilty	relaxed	weak
approval	grateful	resentful	wishful
belittled	happy	responsible	worried
bored	hopeful	sad	
carefree	humiliated	secure	
cautious	hurt	self-controlled	
cheerful	indecisive	shy	
competent	inferior	stressed	
confident	insecure	strong	
confused	involved	superior	
contented	irresponsible	suppressed	
daring	jealous	suspicious	
decisive	joyous	tense	
dependent	lonely	tired	
depressed	loved	trusting	
discontented	lustful	unattractive	

INTENSITY

Those of you who love high-quality music will be aware of how important it is that your equipment picks up the various tones of the music, for example bass, treble and so on. The same is true of quality communication. In order to do an effective job of reflecting feeling and phrases you have to try to mirror the intensity of clients' feelings and expressions by rewording. For example, Cheb has just had a negative experience about which he might feel 'destroyed' (strong intensity), 'upset' (moderate intensity) or 'put out' (weak intensity). Poor communication takes place if you receive accurate language but at inaccurate intensity.

GROUP ACTIVITY 2 (10–15 MINS)

LEVELS OF INTENSITY

● Everyone in the group is included in this exercise.

● Each group member needs a piece of paper, a felt-tip pen and a pin.

● Look at the feeling words listed in the box above and choose one of them. Then choose a level of intensity: *strong*, *moderate* or *weak*. Print these on a piece of paper; this is your own emotional label for this session. You should have something which looks like either of these examples:

- *Fearful: strong intensity.*

- *Envious: moderate intensity.*

- Spend the next few minutes rehearsing individually a sentence or two which reflects the feeling you have chosen and its intensity. For example, for *'Fearful: strong intensity'* you might rehearse, *'I am absolutely terrified of what you will say to me'*.

- All the members of the group help each other to pin their own labels on their own backs. Slowly everybody walks around the room and stops one by one to 'meet' each other's feelings. When you meet somebody else, say your sentence; s/he should guess the feeling and the level of intensity from your sentence and the tone in which you deliver it. S/he then repeats the process for her/his own emotion.

GROUP FEEDBACK

The exercise continues for about ten minutes until you have encountered a variety of different feelings. The whole group reassembles and discusses the following:

- Which emotions were easy to guess? Who was particularly effective?

- What was it like trying to fit feeling with the right intensity level?

- What did the exercise feel like for you?

EMPATHY: REFLECTING FEELINGS

Empathy truly begins only at the point when we can leave behind what we ourselves might feel or think and move into what the speaker might be feeling or thinking.

On this view empathy needs to move from initial listening to oneself to finding out more information which enables me to ask myself, What are they feeling in their situation?
Jacobs, Swift to Hear (1985)

Michael Jacobs clearly sets out the foundations for true empathy. This is about moving to consider what the client is saying and not majoring on how your own experience can show you to understand what s/he is saying. It is dangerous to assume that because you have gone through similar situations your empathy is therefore guaranteed. No situation is ever identical and no two people are alike. The background to a person's life, her/his emotional make-up, depth of experience and anxiety all make empathy a difficult quality to achieve.

Empathy should not be confused with sympathy. It is not feeling sorry for or caring for someone else. It is the ability to move somewhat into the world, thought and feelings of someone else. Empathy is almost always a tentative attempt to put into words what the other person is feeling.

Here are three ground rules for developing empathy with other people. Use them in the exercise below.

GROUND RULE 1

Learn to clarify your 'guess' at what the person is feeling. For example: 'Do you think you are feeling fearful as well as frustrated by…?'

GROUND RULE 2

Wait for more information and confirmation from the speaker before making an empathic response.

GROUND RULE 3

Design your empathic response so that the person can choose to disagree if you make a mistake. For example: 'You seem to be suffering great distress from this but I wonder also whether there's not a lot of resentment and anger. Would you like us to explore this?'

Use of open-ended words and phrases, such as 'perhaps', 'would you', 'I'm not certain but I suspect', can enable the client to think for her/himself about the accuracy of your comments. There are some people who will agree with whatever is said to them, because they lack either the confidence or the ability to make their own progress. The effective and caring counsellor is not trying to give answers or define the issues but to draw the other person out so that accurate communication takes place and you know what you are dealing with. For example:

Counsellor: *I am wondering whether you are bitter about being turned down for promotion.*

Client: *I'm not certain but I would say that I feel quite angry rather than bitter.*

SELF-EVALUATION

PRACTISING EMPATHY

Below are a number of situations which you can use for practising empathic responses. Using the ground rules above work your way through them and think about what you would say in response to each statement. After you have done this evaluate your responses. Which situation was the hardest to respond to? Which was the easiest? Why? Would you like to rewrite your attempts? How would you improve them?

☺ I have just heard that I am to be made redundant and the hope of another job is very unlikely.

☺ My son is getting into more and more trouble at school, he's so badly behaved, and I feel so ashamed when I have to go to the school and face the teachers.

☺ We had saved all year for that holiday and now the company we booked with has gone bust. It's the last straw.

☺ My dearest friend died last week in an air crash.

☺ I can't believe it. Just when I thought my job was going nowhere I've been promoted to a senior position.

☺ I recently became a Christian and now my boyfriend won't have anything to do with me. He says it's weird, all that kind of stuff.

☺ I've tried again and again to gain access to my daughter in the family court but even when I was granted parental rights by a court order, they didn't enforce it. The child's mother just keeps on breaking the law and nobody will do anything about it.

☺ It's wonderful you know. At last my short stories have been accepted for publication and I feel on top of the world.

☺ My wife has just given birth to a lovely baby girl. It's our first.

☺ I hate being single. I long for someone who will love me but I guess it will never happen.

PERSONAL REFLECTION

Answer these questions for your own information and self-awareness:

● Do you empathize with your own feelings, or do you blame or criticize yourself for them?

● Are you someone who can identify a range of feelings in your own experience, or only a few? How do you think your own perceptions about feelings could influence the counselling situation?

● If while counselling you were to find yourself getting emotional about someone else's problem what would you do?

Personal Diary

EXPRESSING FEELINGS
THE ART OF EXPRESSING EMOTION

Many people find it difficult to put their feelings into words. Many of us have been brought up in families and schools where feeling is devalued. How often have we heard phrases like this?

- *Don't be angry.*

- *Cheer up! There's no need to look so sad.*

- *Big boys don't cry.*

- *Grin and bear it!*

It has been pointed out that the language of Sanskrit is reputed to have more than 900 words in which to express feeling states but English has fewer than fifty. Nevertheless, being able to express our feelings in appropriate and productive ways is a crucial part of being psychologically healthy:

To experience emotions and express them to another person is not only a major source of joy, it is also necessary for your psychological well-being. It is natural to have feelings. The capacity to feel is as much a part of being a person as the capacity to think and reason.
Johnson (1981)

In this unit we build on the work that you did in Unit 4.1. Expressing and reflecting feelings go together but they are both distinct skills in themselves.

✔ AIMS

The aims of this unit are:

- To explore the process by which feeling is expressed.

- To look at the role that clear expression of feeling plays in male-female relationships.

- To identify a variety of effective ways to communicate feelings.

STARTER ACTIVITY (10 MINS)

EVERYDAY FEELINGS
This exercise focuses on expressing feelings verbally.

- **Individually, for three minutes go through the events of this last week and note down any feelings that were memorable—either high or low. Then think about whether you expressed any of these feelings to other people and how you did this. Jot down the incidents.**

- **Get into groups of two and three and share your own list with the others in your group. Listen carefully to each other. Expressing feelings can be difficult. It is important that as a small group you establish a sense of confidentiality and trust.**

GROUP FEEDBACK
Discuss together just how easy and how hard it was for you to express yourselves.

SUPPRESSING FEELINGS: THE ENEMY OF INTERPERSONAL RELATIONSHIPS

It is now generally believed that suppressing feelings can contribute to forms of psychosomatic illness, for example migraines and ulcers, and may even contribute to forms of cancer. Views such as these about the effects of suppression are notoriously difficult to support with hard, tangible fact but there are other effects which are more clearly visible.

Consider for a moment the role feelings can have in your friendships and relationships. Have you ever experienced suppressing your own feelings? What happened? Was it for the good or was it unhelpful in the long run? Below is a situation where the suppression of true feelings led to conflicts and barriers between a married couple.

CASE STUDY: JENNY AND SEAN

Jenny and Sean were newly married and deeply in love with each other. They had been married for about three months when Sean announced that he would be going to a rock concert with his brother Ken who had somehow managed to acquire the tickets. Jenny was not pleased with this. She had not been consulted about the concert and, what is more, she had a dim view of being left on her own for the evening. When she told Sean how she felt, he replied, 'But we agreed to go together eight months ago—long before we were married—we've always gone to concerts together. As brothers we're close.' His response made no difference to Jenny. She was quick to condemn Ken's thoughtlessness in not getting three tickets so that they could all go.

Sean was left with a decision: should he cancel going to the concert and let his brother down, or should he go and upset his wife? He spoke to Ken on the phone and carefully hinted that it was difficult for Jenny, who thought she should have been invited. His brother was more concerned not to cause any hassle for Sean so he assured him that if he pulled out it would be all right by him. As it happened, Sean chose to go. And that is where feelings began to be suppressed and relationships began to be eroded.

THE RELATIONSHIP BETWEEN JENNY AND SEAN

Sean never really expressed to his wife his feelings of concern, disappointment and anger that she should find fault with him simply because he wished to share an evening out with his brother. Instead he held those feelings in. But a barrier had appeared in the marriage. He was less likely to tell Jenny about other meetings because this one had caused so many problems. He would have to limit the times he spent with Ken on his own. Ken still sometimes insisted on seeing his brother alone for a drink or a concert, but would have to find outlets elsewhere.

THE RELATIONSHIP BETWEEN JENNY AND KEN

Jenny subsequently held resentment against Ken for being so insensitive and excluding her from the evening. But she never expressed anything to him. This made him feel unwelcome when he occasionally visited their house. Before one visit, Ken was delayed for over an hour in traffic en route and Jenny was so furious that her evening alone with Sean had been delayed that she stayed in the kitchen for the entire visit under the pretext of cooking. Sean could not help noticing but he said nothing. Ken was astonished at this behaviour and this fixed in him the idea that his brother had married a very possessive woman. His view of Jenny was very poor. Nothing was resolved. More barriers were raised. Feelings continued to be forced inwards.

THE RELATIONSHIP BETWEEN SEAN AND KEN

This took the largest blow. Ken felt so unwelcome and awkward whenever he visited that he began to come less often. He regretted this bitterly but could not see a viable alternative. If he expressed his feelings of rejection and hurt, and his sense of loss about the relationship with his brother he might cause hassle between the married couple. On one occasion he gathered courage and started to allude to Jenny's behaviour to his brother but Sean could not handle it: 'She can't help it, it's her background. She's so insecure and we have an agreement not to speak about each other to other people. That would be disloyal.' Ken was silenced. He did not want to alienate his brother even further. The feelings were suppressed and so was the relationship they both treasured.

This case study shows the effects on a family relationship if feelings are not expressed. If you want to be effective in solving interpersonal problems you need all the relevant information (including feelings) that you can get. This means that your feelings need to be conscious, discussable and controllable.

GROUP ACTIVITY 1 (15 MINS)

COUNSELLING SEAN, JENNY OR KEN

This is an activity you can do individually or in small groups. Make sure that you record the main points for future reference so that you can refer to them again.

Select one of the three characters from the above case study (Sean, Jenny or Ken) to counsel. Imagine that this character has come to you as a counsellor for help. Follow these guidelines in deciding what you would do:

- **Define the problem from the client's perspective.**

- **Explore the issues that arise out of the problem. Identify any skills s/he may need to work on in order to manage this problem.**

- **Look at the options the client has and the time span s/he might feel comfortable with in making changes.**

- **Plan working goals with your client.**

SUPPRESSING YOUR FEELINGS AND YOUR PERCEPTIONS

Denying your feelings can result in selective perception. When feelings are unresolved your perceptions of situations and information can be affected. For example, if you are denying your anger, you may perceive accurately all hostile actions from others but be blind to their warmth and friendliness. Unresolved feelings tend to widen such blind spots.

Suppressing your feelings can cause your judgments to be biased. It is common knowledge that people often refuse to accept a good idea because someone they dislike suggested it. Conversely, they accept bad ideas because someone they like devised them. Just look at the way people cast their political vote! Aggressive advertising firms know this and promote the person rather than the politics. If you are aware of your feelings and manage them constructively, the chances of your being more unbiased and objective in your judgments are increased.

DISTORTED WAYS OF EXPRESSING FEELINGS

Expressing your feelings is a necessary skill which, like any other skill, needs to be acquired. Distortions obscure real communication. They make it difficult for other people to respond and, as a result, communication is halted or simply breaks down. Johnson (1981) lists eight distorted ways in which people communicate their emotions:

- *Labels:* 'You are rude, hostile, and self-centred,' = 'When you interrupt me I get angry.'

- *Commands:* 'Shut up!' = 'I'm annoyed at what you just said.'

- *Questions:* 'Are you always this crazy?' = 'When you do not pay attention to me I feel left out.'

- *Sarcasm:* 'I'm glad you are early!' = 'You are late; it has delayed our work and that irritates me.'

- *Approval:* 'You are wonderful!' = 'I like you.'

- *Disapproval:* 'You are terrible!' = 'I do not like you.'

- *Name calling:* 'You are a creep!' = 'You are embarrassing me.'

EXPRESSING FEELINGS IN MALE-FEMALE COMMUNICATION

The need to express feelings appropriately is seen dramatically in the area of marital and male-female relationships. Research into divorce statistics shows that 70 per cent of women initiate divorce against men. Relate counsellors and other family therapists report that their interviews with women who have initiated divorce reveal interesting reasons why they have taken this step. Their interviews show that the primary reason women have for divorcing men is not for committing adultery. It is because they are deeply disappointed that their husbands have been unable to communicate with them at any meaningful level:

Whenever I ask him how he is, he just says OK or he tells me what's been happening at work. I want to know how he feels, whether he's happy, or frustrated or hopeful. I wanted him to trust me with where he was at and then I would have felt that we have a relationship. But he just kept telling me that I expected too much from him.

When I married Tony I was full of love and excitement because we got on so well and I felt I had a wonderful friend as well as a lover. I had to find out the hard way. He never ever talks to me. The most I ever get out of him is when he asks me about the kids or what I did today or he makes a comment about his car or the television programme he's watching. He never talks about himself. He could be clinically depressed and I never would have known it.

I have just cried and cried because he never tells me he loves me. At first I tried, I asked him why he never said how he felt about me. He got really stroppy and said it was obvious he loved me wasn't it? He said that he worked hard and paid for everything and he had built me a new kitchen and taken me where I wanted to go on holiday and that showed he loved me didn't it? He said I was never satisfied. I felt starved of the affection I needed. For me the words aren't just important, they are the way I know I am loved.

Remarks like these show that for many women the expression of feelings by their male partner is a central issue. It would be interesting to interview the men in these different situations and to get their perceptions of the same situations. Of course, it is reductive to stereotype all women as needing verbal expressions of love or all men as being non-expressive of their feelings. However, the male-female differences listed elsewhere in this book have all been identified by a variety of authors and thinkers; I cite them here not as proof of a point of view but as trigger material to get us to think through the important issue of what makes effective male-female communication.

For those of you reading this book who are Christians this is crucial. Statistics show that the divorce rate for churchgoing Christians is the same as the overall national rate: one in three marriages ends in divorce. The figure is already rising; it is estimated that divorce will end one in two marriages by the end of the century.

GROUP ACTIVITY 2 (10 MINS)

DISCUSSION

- How do you observe care and love taking place in your community? Do women show care by their questions, verbal concern, expressions of affection and affirmation? Do men show their love and care by actions, for example by fixing/paying for things, offering to carry or move something? What does your group think? Is it simply that men are misunderstood and that their actions rather than their words portray their feelings? Or is there a real lack of ability or will to express themselves?

- Can you think of instances where a single message may be communicated in two ways: in actions and in words? For instance, the enquiry 'How are you?' may be conveyed by a man as a hand on the shoulder or an arm around it.

PERSONAL REFLECTION

QUESTIONNAIRE:
MALE-FEMALE COMMUNICATION

Remember our work in Unit 2.2 about the communication process? Men and women may both use the same words but they do not necessarily exchange the same meanings when they do so. Below is a short questionnaire. Select the responses which are closest to your own.

What do your answers tell you about your personal beliefs about men and women?

1. When a man or a woman does practical work, for example painting the home or cooking a meal, is this an expression of love and affection? Do you:

   (a) Value it as much as words?

   (b) Prefer occasional verbal messages of love?

   (c) Require frequent verbal messages of love?

2. Would you prefer your partner to give you:

   (a) A practical gift that you really wanted, for example a new dishwasher, a set of screwdrivers?

   (b) A bouquet of your favourite flowers?

   (c) A special meal with romance and candlelight?

3. Do you find the need to respond with words when someone pays you a compliment? If someone pays you regular compliments do you find this:

   (a) A pleasure?

   (b) A pressure?

   (c) Don't mind?

4. How would you feel if your partner (or future partner) forgot your anniversary/birthday? Would you:

   (a) Think that you weren't valued and loved?

   (b) Feel disappointed?

   (c) Assume some other explanation?

5. Your partner/younger brother/sister/best friend is very late home. When s/he returns, are you:

   (a) Angry and upset because s/he has not phoned?

   (b) All right because you have assumed s/he could not get to a phone?

   (c) Just grateful that s/he is safe?

SELF-EVALUATION

This exercise is an opportunity for you to explore your own feelings and to evaluate your responses. Which of the following feelings are the most difficult and the easiest for you to express:

☺ ambition;

☺ leadership;

☺ assertion;

☺ vulnerability;

☺ sensitivity;

☺ affection;

☺ anger;

☺ lack of confidence.

Think of situations where you have faced any of these feelings. What happened? How would you like things to change? What steps could possibly lead to change?

WHAT COUPLES SAY
ABOUT EXPRESSING FEELINGS

A recent poll carried out by the BBC on couples revealed some interesting results and percentages:

ON FEELINGS

● 64 per cent said they should instinctively know how each other are feeling.

ON COMMUNICATION

● 85 per cent said they were dissatisfied with the relationship.

● 42 per cent said they had repetitive circular arguments.

● 87 per cent said they were arguing more than once a week.

ON MUTUAL WORKLOAD

● 15 per cent said they would hand over the work to their partner.

● 47 per cent said they would rather share the work equally.

ON THE MOST COMMON
PROBLEMS BETWEEN COUPLES

1. Money.

2. Household chores.

3. Children.

4. Sex.

ON SPENDING TIME WITH EACH OTHER

● 38 per cent had not spent any time alone with their partner in the past week.

HELPING PEOPLE TO
MANAGE THEIR FEELINGS

Many people come for help wanting release from painful and negative feelings. Often they are subject to feelings such as strong anger, depression, listlessness or apathy. Here we look at one model for would-be counsellors to explore in helping people manage feelings. You can find this model in the book *Practical Counselling and Helping Skills* by Richard Nelson-Jones (1993). You will recall that previous units in this book have looked at several of these skills and issues.

ILLUSTRATIVE THINKING AND
ACTION SKILLS FOR MANAGING DEPRESSION

THINKING SKILLS

☺ Possessing realistic personal rules.

☺ Perceiving others and self accurately.

☺ Attributing cause accurately.

☺ Predicting realistically.

☺ Setting limits and saying 'no'.

ACTION SKILLS

☺ Relationship skills.

☺ Initiating contact.

☺ Self-disclosing.

☺ Assertion skills.

☺ Pleasant activities skills.

Richard Nelson-Jones expands the above points:

- **Possessing realistic personal rules:** clients can create and sustain their depressed feelings when striving to attain and failing to live up to unrealistic rules. These include 'I must be perfect' and 'I must always gain others' approval.'

- **Perceiving others and self accurately:** depressed clients tend to jump to negative conclusions about how others perceive them and are skilled at blocking out positive information about themselves.

- **Attributing cause accurately:** depressed clients may both overemphasize their responsibility for negative events and attribute them more than is warranted to stable and global causes.

- **Predicting realistically:** depressed clients tend to predict the future negatively. They are more prone to feelings of hopelessness, helplessness and perceived self-inefficacy than non-depressed people.

Nelson-Jones suggests that the client will need to develop three areas of supportive skills to help her/himself manage depression:

- **Relationship skills:** depressed clients are lonely because they have too few, as well as insufficiently high-quality, social contacts. Initiating contact and appropriate self-disclosing are among the relationship skills needed.

- **Assertion skills:** frequently depressed clients lower their self-esteem through inability to be assertive. For instance, depressed clients who do not stand up for themselves may feel doubly bad.

- **Pleasant activities skills:** as the old adage says, 'A little of what you fancy does you good.' Depressed clients can develop skills of identifying activities they find rewarding.

Personal Diary

What happens when you constantly have to work or live with someone who is very different from yourself? For example, if you are a quiet reserved person and your flatmate/partner/close colleague/workmate turns out to be a loud, vivacious, non-stop talker (or vice versa), what do you do? Do you grin and bear it? Do you try and avoid her/him more and more? Do you have a confrontation and insist that s/he becomes more like you? Or do you do something different?

Take another situation. You are someone who likes to plan way ahead of time for occasions/holidays/going out with someone. You like to know when, how, what and where. You are organized. Your husband/wife/ partner/friend turns out to be the exact opposite. For her/him to be organized much ahead of time is like tyranny. S/he hates being tied down. You are continually frustrated when s/he will not meet your deadlines, when s/he is late for appointments or fails to give you advance warning of what s/he is doing. Differences like these can result in relational crisis.

Jung's model of typology is a very valuable resource for any counsellor as it is one way of understanding differences between people. It is not a method of character analysis nor is it intended to fit people into 'boxes' or label them, but it seeks to find out your preferences and the things which make you 'you'.

✔ AIMS

Our aims in this unit are:

● To give a basic knowledge of Jung's theory of psychological types.

● To look at how his various categories of introvert/extrovert, sensing/intuitive, feeling/thinking show themselves in the differences of personality that people have.

STARTER ACTIVITY(10–15 MINS)

INTROVERTS AND EXTROVERTS

Look at the following statements and decide which of them you prefer. Even if you can only register a small preference try to find it and score yourself.

1. **When you are at a party, do you tend to:**

   (a) Talk to a variety of people including strangers?

   (b) Interact with a few people whom you already know?

2. **In your social group, do you tend to:**

   (a) Be up to the mark with everyone's news?

   (b) Get behind on knowing what is happening?

3. **When you are in company with others, do you tend to:**

   (a) Start conversations with others?

   (b) Wait to be approached by others?

4. **Do you prefer to:**

   (a) Have many friends but see them less often?

   (b) Have very few friends and see them more often?

5. **When the phone rings, do you:**

   (a) Get a move on hoping to answer first?

   (b) Secretly hope that someone else will answer?

6. **Do you consider yourself to be someone who is:**

   (a) Easily approachable by others?

   (b) Somewhat reserved?

Now look at your scores. If you scored mostly or all (a)s then you tend towards being an extrovert. If you scored mostly or all (b)s then you tend towards being an introvert. (This is not a reliable measure but it should give you some sort of indication of preference.)

JUNG AND PERSONALITY TYPES

Jung's model is concerned with the way in which you habitually prefer to function in relation to the outside world. Jung differentiates various typological groups:

- There are two personality attitudes: **introversion** and **extroversion**.

- There are four functions: **thinking, sensation, intuition** and **feeling.** Each of these may operate in an introverted or extroverted way.

The result is **eight variations** with detailed descriptions of how each of the functions appears either in the introverted or in the extroverted attitude. What follows here is a brief explanation of the terms Jung used.

INTROVERSION AND EXTROVERSION

Jung classified people into types. He made 'introvert' and 'extrovert' household words, but he also wrote about the psychological qualities associated with these attitudes:

- **Introverts get their energy from within.** They usually prefer quiet and reflection, times of privacy and are interested in ideas. Intoverts are essentially conservative, and prefer the familiarity of home. Their social lives err on the side of intimacy with a few close friends.

- **Extroverts get their energy from being outgoing.** They usually prefer the external world of places, people and facts. They like to travel, to meet new people and to see lots of new places. They are adventurous, and tend to be open and friendly. In the extroverted attitude, external factors are the dominant motivating force for judgments, perceptions, feelings and action.

Jung made the point that introverts and extroverts can have set views of each other:

- To the introvert, who tends to be more self-sufficient than the extrovert, an extrovert might appear superficial, over-friendly and 'gushing', someone who gads about.

- To the extrovert, an introverted person might be seen as a stick-in-the-mud, who tends to be dull and predictable, staying on home ground.

No one, of course, is only introverted or only extroverted. Although each of us develops one attitude more than the other, the opposite attitude is still potentially present.

The important factor in determining your own type as introvert or extrovert does not rest on what you do but rather on your motivation for doing it, that is, the direction in which your energy naturally flows. For the introvert the subject, that is, their inner world, is the most important thing. For the extrovert the object, that is, the outside world, is interesting and attractive.

Understanding your natural preference for introversion or extroversion can help you to identify certain levels of personal stress. Take the case study of Gerald, for example.

CASE STUDY: GERALD,
AN EXTROVERT IN AN INTROVERTED JOB

At school Gerald was a high achiever. He went from one academic success to another until finally he passed his entrance exams in mathematics for Oxford University. At university he showed himself to be a thorough all-rounder—he was popular with lots of friends, he rowed for the college team and he also excelled in his studies and graduated with a first-class degree. As is typical of so many graduates he was at a loss to know what to do when he left university. His father encouraged him to go into the same profession as himself: accountancy. Gerald was immediately snapped up by a city firm anxious to have his talent.

Most of his days he spent poring over commercial accounts and dealing with paperwork; his exposure to people was minimal. Anxious to do well, he often worked long hours, but this work was almost always on his own as well, so his social life declined. After three months with the firm, Gerald started to get depressed. After six months his energy and natural vitality for life were drained, although his work was first-rate. The firm were impressed and raised his salary. Everyone was pleased with him but he was not pleased with himself. He knew that things could not go on as they were. He was not himself any more.

It was his old girlfriend Lucy who came to his rescue. 'You know why you're so miserable,' she said, 'It's because you're in the wrong job—you're a people person, you always have been since I've known you, and all you do all day is work with facts and figures.' This insight clicked with Gerald and he decided to ask his boss whether he might be given more of the client work in which he had to meet and hold discussions with other people. His boss agreed, although client work of this sort was usually given to more senior staff and the decision was a risk. The risk was rewarded. Clients were delighted with both

Gerald's professionalism and his personality. Gerald had been counselled well, not by a counsellor but, like many people, by the perceptions of an old and trusted friend.

It could have been so different. His rise in salary and the financial security it gave him may have kept Gerald in a job that drained him and worked against his personality. Gerald as an extrovert was caught in a job which was more suited to someone with a preference for introversion interested in their own calculations, space, time and privacy. He preferred to be involved with people and their situation, and he gained his energy from this.

In practice, it is impossible to demonstrate introversion and extroversion in isolation from the four functions. Each of these, we will see, has its special area of expertise.

GROUP ACTIVITY 1 (15 MINS)

IMPROVING COMMUNICATION
BETWEEN INTROVERTS AND EXTROVERTS

- **Everyone reads the characteristics of introversion and extroversion below.**

- **Each person makes an attempt to judge her/his own preference for introvert or extrovert. Even if the preference is slight, it is still to be counted.**

- **The group leader asks all the extroverts to raise a hand and, as far as possible, they are grouped with the introverts in twos or threes so that the groups are mixed.**

- **The groups discuss between themselves the following issues:**

  - **What do introverts find difficult about extroverts and vice versa?**

  - **How does your preference affect your daily relationships with others?**

■ Does your main employment/work situation favour introverts or extroverts, or neither?

■ Think of someone close to you that you suspect shares a different preference. What would you like her/him to understand about you?

CHARACTERISTICS OF INTROVERSION AND EXTROVERSION

If you are an introvert you probably:

☺ Enjoy quiet and privacy.

☺ Often respond to enquiries from others with 'I'll come back to you later' or 'Give me time to think about that'.

☺ Feel that others take advantage of your ability to listen to them.

☺ Often wish that you could get your opinion known more forcefully than you do.

☺ Need to 'recharge your batteries' on you own after you have spent time with other people or in a group.

If you are an extrovert you probably:

☺ Talk first, think later.

☺ Like to include as many people as possible in your activities.

☺ Are easy to talk to but can be somewhat dominating in a conversation.

☺ Prefer discussing things in a group rather than thinking about them by yourself.

☺ Find listening more difficult than talking.

☺ Need approval from colleagues/partners/others for who you are.

Until you hear you are doing a good job you do not quite believe it.

☺ Get suspicious if people are too free with their words and compliment you.

GROUP FEEDBACK

The whole group reassembles and pools its perceptions about how introversion and extroversion influence their church or their community.

THE FOUR FUNCTIONS

Jung identifies four functions, each of which has its special area of expertise: **sensation** (or sensing); **intuition** (or intuitive); **thinking**; and **feeling**.

SENSATION

This refers to **perception by means of the physical sense organs**. People who have a definite preference for sensing get their information or perception from the senses: touch, sight, hearing and so on. They believe that the most important thing is the present moment and they think that 'seeing is believing'. They are happiest when there is concrete evidence for what they think.

If you are a sensate, you probably:

● Like to live for what is happening now and not think about tomorrow or next week.

● Prefer to work with facts and figures rather than ideas and theories.

● Get frustrated when you are not given clear instructions; you hate 'guidelines'.

● Read books or magazines from the beginning to the end.

● Enjoy work which is practical and which has some practical outcome.

● Think that 'seeing is believing' rather than depending on imagination or possibility.

INTUITION

This refers to **perception by way of the unconscious**. People who show a distinct preference for intuition get their information from what they do not see and touch. They prefer to rely on hunches, inspiration, their own intuition and a 'sixth sense' about things. They are happiest when there are lots of possibilities to be thought about.

If you are an intuitive, you probably:

● Think about several things at once.

● Are accused of being absent-minded.

● Find future possibilities more exciting than present realities.

● Are interested in the meaning of things rather than the bare facts.

● Find routine difficult and boring.

● Prefer to imagine your next year's holiday than book it straight away.

GROUP ACTIVITY 2 (10–15 MINS)

SENSING AND INTUITION

How do you feel about your preference for sensation or intuition? What kind of interpersonal problems do you think are most frequent between sensates and intuitives? How might this difference affect the following situations?

● **The way you perform at a job interview.**

● **The way people prefer to worship.**

Get into small groups of two or three and discuss these issues.

FEELING AND THINKING

FEELING

This refers to **the function of subjective judgment or valuation**. The person who shows a distinct preference for feeling prefers to make decisions based on human values. What other people feel and think about what is proposed is of prime importance to them. If you are a feeler, you probably:

● Overwork yourself to meet other people's needs, even at your own expense.

● Try to sense how others are feeling.

● Ask questions at meetings such as, 'How will this affect those people?'

● Prefer things to be harmonious even at the expense of clarity.

● Get embarrassed and stressed when there is conflict.

THINKING

This refers to **the process of cognitive thought**. Thinking people are those who prefer to decide according to logic and analysis first and foremost. If you are a thinker, you will probably:

● Base a dispute on what is fair rather than what will please others.

● Tell people you disagree with them so that they will not think they are right.

● Believe things when you have sufficient evidence and information to decide.

● Think it is more important to be right than liked.

GROUP ACTIVITY 3 (10 MINS)

In groups of two to four people discuss the following issues. One of you should volunteer to jot down notes of the discussion and feed back to the whole group when the course coordinator draws you together.

● **What problems might a feeling person have if s/he were in an intimate relationship with a thinking person?**

- **What accusations and misunderstandings do you think exist because of these differences?**

Group feedback
The whole group reassembles and pools its conclusions.

Rational and irrational
Jung described two of the four functions, thinking and feeling, as **rational** and the other two functions, sensation and intuition, as **irrational** (this does not mean illogical but rather beyond or outside of reason).

The ideal, according to Jung, occurs when a person has conscious access to all four functions equally so that s/he can meet a variety of circumstances in life with a variety of personal strengths. But in practice the four functions are not equally available to us in conscious thought. Invariably one function or the other is more developed. As a result:

- The function you are most likely to use is called the **primary function** (not because it is 'better' but because you are most likely to use it).

- The function you are most likely to use second is called the **auxiliary function**. In practice, the auxiliary function is always one whose nature (rational or irrational) is different from the primary function. So, for instance, feeling cannot be the secondary function when thinking is dominant because both are rational functions. Either of the irrational functions can be auxiliary to either of the rational functions and vice versa.

- The function you are least likely to use is called the **inferior function**.

The relationships between functions are shown in the diagram on the right.

Jung believed that most people have one dominating type although some people can show two or even three. Below we introduce you to four of the eight types that Jung identifies. This is only a sample of his thinking. To complete the picture you would need to look at extroverted sensing and extroverted intuition, introverted feeling and introverted thinking. But if you can identify the principles upon which he builds you will probably be able to construct the other types yourself. If in doubt, refer to Jung's work *Psychological Types* (1971) or, for a synopsis, Daryl Sharp's *Personality Types* (1987).

Extroversion and two functions: thinking and feeling

The extroverted thinking type
If your actions mainly proceed from intellectually considered thoughts then you are a thinking type. If you combine this with an orientation towards the outer world of people, places and things, then, according to Jung, you are an **extroverted thinking type**.

Extroverted thinkers are good at establishing order. They are logical, with a good sense of facts. They can bring clarity into emotional situations and they tend to be a very real asset on any committee where a

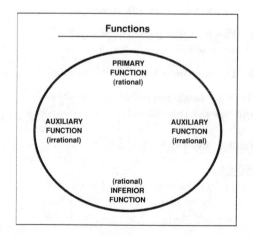

knowledge of rules or procedures is important. At their worst they can be religious zealots, sticklers for the rules. According to Jung, extreme extroverted thinking types bring both themselves and others over to their prescribed 'formula' for life: a system of rules, ideals and principles. For them justice and truth are absolutes based on what they consider to be 'objective reality'. Their language has lots of 'oughts' and 'shoulds' in it.

The function most in opposition to thinking is feeling. So, for extroverted thinkers their **introverted feeling will be inferior**. This means that certain aspects of their lives—artistic sense, cultivating close friendships, family time and priorities, relationships of love and so on—can suffer. This does not mean that extroverted thinkers do not feel deeply—their feeling may be very strong but it does not flow outward towards their loved ones. The feeling is all within them. Inferior introverted feeling types often comes across as cold and unfriendly. From their point of view, however, they are more interested in the facts than in what effect their attitude may have on others.

THE EXTROVERTED FEELING TYPE

Without this type a polite social life would be almost impossible because collective expressions of culture depend on the **extroverted feeling type**. Extroverted feeling takes people to concerts, to church, on company trips away, to birthday parties; it sends anniversary cards and remembers Father's Day.

Extroverted feeling types usually find it easy to make friends because they can quickly work out what the outer situation requires— they may compliment their friends on their new car or the dress/suit they are wearing. They may not even like the dress or suit themselves but they are quick to see that the wearer needs approval or acceptance and they give it. Except in extreme cases, the feelings

they give out have a personal quality and their conversations are genuine, even though the subjective factor is very much suppressed. The image of an extroverted feeling type is that of someone who is well adjusted both to the place they are in, and the people and the social values that surround her/him.

Jung gives one description of a typical woman whose preference is extroverted feeling:

The 'suitable' man is loved, and no one else; he is suitable not because he appeals to her hidden subjective nature—about which she usually knows nothing—but because he comes up to all reasonable expectations in the matter of age, position, income, size and respectability of his family etc… The love feeling of this type of woman… is genuine and not just shrewd… There are countless 'reasonable' marriages of this kind and they are by no means the worst. These women are good companions and excellent mothers so long as the husbands and children are blessed with the conventional psychic constitution.

Psychological Types *(1971)*

The inferior for an extroverted feeling type is **introverted thinking** so there is a danger of being overwhelmed by the social world out there—the traditional and generally accepted standard—and thus losing sight of her/his own subjective thoughts about what is going on inside. Extreme feeling types do not have to think about what someone or something means to them, they just *know*.

People of this type can have negative thoughts about the very persons most valued by their feelings. When extroverted feelers are depressed they tend to abandon their outer world and introvert; then they are often subject to morose thoughts about themselves. This can happen especially when they are on their own. A typical extroverted feeler then rushes out to meet a friend or abandons her/himself to watching TV in an effort to crowd out the inner world.

THE INTROVERTED SENSING TYPE

Introverted sensing types use their favourite process, sensing, in their inner life which gives them almost unshakeable ideas. They do not enter into anything impulsively but when they have committed themselves to an action or line of thought they are very hard to budge. Introverted sensates make a habit of comparing present and past situations. They are cautious about any new changes and they like everything to be kept factual, and stated clearly and simply.

The inferior for introverted sensates is **extroverted intuition**. They can therefore be overwhelmed by too much change and flux in their personal circumstance without the necessary factual evidence to back it up. Unlike extroverted sensate types, who sense intuitions that concern the subject (that is, themselves), introverted sensates are more inclined to feel dark, dangerous possibilities hovering over life in the outside world. They often fear for their loved ones or for the world at large.

THE INTROVERTED INTUITIVE TYPE

The introverted intuitive type (like the extroverted intuitive type) has a capacity for seeing future possibilities. But this intuition is directed inwards so introverted intuitives are often found among poets, artists, prophets, counsellors and psychologists. Because people of this type are often exploring the possibilities of the inner self they are especially liable to neglect ordinary physical demands. In fact, they often have little awareness of their own bodily needs. They can easily be misunderstood because introverted intuitives are characteristically vague about details in the 'real' world. They may get lost in a strange place, they lose things, they can double-book or forget appointments, even run out of clean clothes. They do not relate to outer facts but to inner images. Jung, however, also saw the value of this type to the community:

... these images represent possible views of the world which may give life a new potential, this function, which to the outside world is the strangest of all, is... indispensable to the psychic life of a people. Had this type not existed, there would have been no prophets in Israel.

The inferior for this type is **extroverted sensation**. This gives rise to compensatory extroverted sensation of what Jung called 'a low and primitive order'. It would be consistent with Jung's thought to say that by repressing their sensation introverted sensates often find it unconsciously breaking through into the outer world. For example, a middle-aged intellectual or academic may be suddenly bowled over by a passionate love affair.

APPLYING JUNG'S WORK

Today, Jung's work on personality types can be applied to anyone who wants to know and understand her/himself or her/his friends better. The Myers-Briggs Type Indicator is a questionnaire instrument which records the preferences we have. This unit is not a reliable guide to a full personality test; it merely gives you an indication of your own preferences. To get greater accuracy and clarity you would need to do the Myers-Briggs Type Indicator which applies Jung's theory of psychological types. You can get more information about this indicator by reading *Gifts Differing* (1980).

Jung's work has brought enrichment and hope to many many people in the quest for meaning in their lives. In his autobiography Jung wrote, 'Life is—or has—meaning and meaninglessness. I cherish the anxious hope that meaning will preponderate and win the battle.'

PERSONAL REFLECTION

Draw a circle and place in it those people who are close to you among your family or friends. Who do you imagine

are the extroverts and the introverts?
What behaviour of theirs gives you clues
to the type they may be? Have you ever
had any misunderstandings or problems
in your relationships with these different
types? Are there ways these could be
avoided?

Now think of either your workplace
or your church community. What
aspects of work or church life, ministry
or worship would most appeal to (a)
introverts and (b) extroverts? Or does
personality preference have little or
nothing to do with job preference or
spirituality?

SELF-EVALUATION

Look again at this unit and focus on the
different personality aspects:

● the introvert/extrovert;

● the sensate/intuitive;

● the feeler/thinker.

Write a letter to yourself in which you
describe your own thoughts and feelings
about who you are at the present time.
The letter begins 'Dear self'. For
example, you might tell yourself that you
are pleased at the skills you have in
meeting people but that you wish you
had a few deeper relationships rather
than a lot of casual friends. Then write
and inform yourself of the changes you
most deeply desire. You may use this
personal piece of writing for meditation
or prayer or, if you are being
counselled, it may be helpful in focusing
your thinking.

Personal Diary

Module 5

SKILLS OF OBSERVATION, CONFRONTATION AND SELF-DISCLOSURE

5.1 THE ART OF OBSERVATION
NON-VERBAL COMMUNICATION

The messages that your body sends are just as important as the words you use. In order to show attentiveness you need physically to convey your receptiveness and interest. For example, imagine that a lover was declaring her/his personal feelings for you while at the same time looking at her/his watch or looking out of the window in order to see who was approaching. There would be an incongruence. Congruence between both your body and your verbal messages is essential in making yourself understood.

This unit expands on the work covered in Unit 2.2 on listening and attending. Here we focus on the wider issues of non-verbal communication.

✔ AIMS

The aims of this unit are:

- To identify some of the main body messages that show interest and attention.

- To examine the range and use of your voice messages when you communicate.

- To heighten your powers of non-verbal observation.

- To help you to assess your own non-verbal range of skills and to develop them.

STARTER ACTIVITY (5–10 MINS)

SPEAKING WITHOUT WORDS

- **Individually, write a short message of greeting. It should say how you are feeling today/tonight and include a short piece of information about something in the past week which has happened or affected you.**

- **In small groups of three or four practise sending this message to the rest of the group without using sounds or words of any kind. You can use eye movements, expressions, hand movements, body actions— anything except words.**

GROUP FEEDBACK
When everyone has had a turn, give each other feedback in the larger group on how you yourself felt and how others in the group performed.

OBSERVATION: A QUESTION OF INTERPRETATION

We constantly use our powers of observation. All day and every day we are observing the world in which we live. Yet our observation is selective. Think for a minute of all you have seen today? Can you recall every detail or are there moments that are crystal clear, some that are very dim and others that have already faded from memory? As human beings we select not only our memories but also what we see in the world around us. Try the group activity below and see how you get on.

GROUP ACTIVITY 1 (10–15 MINS)

OBSERVATION
This activity requires a leader to keep time and to give instructions. Everyone

needs a clean sheet of paper and a
pen/pencil.

● The leader explains that s/he is going
to give one instruction, that s/he is
going to give it once only and that
there are no questions allowed about
the exercise.

● The leader reads out the instruction:
'Observe and write down what you
observe.'

● After five minutes—not before and
not after—the leader stops the group.

● Group members are asked one by
one (depending on time) to read out
to the rest of the group what they
wrote down.

● The following questions are raised:

 ■ How did different people interpret
 the word 'observe'?

 ■ Did they stick to visible features
 only?

 ■ Did they include what they heard
 and felt?

 ■ Did they observe things that were
 not 'there'?

 ■ What were the different selections
 like?

The scientist Karl Popper used to give this
activity to his students to show that a degree
of personal interpretation was present in all
so-called 'neutral' observations.

OBSERVING AND
SENDING POSITIVE BODY MESSAGES

YOUR ATTITUDE: 'I'M TOO BUSY'

Counsellors are sometimes perceived as being
unable to help others because they give out
the message **'I'm too busy'**. Of course this is
never actually said in words but all sorts of
signals can give this message. You may fail to
let others know you are available. You may
show visible signs of being overworked, for
example by always rushing everywhere with
never a moment to stop. And then there are
the signals you give out to specific
individuals. You may physically edge away
from someone who is wishing to discuss
personal concerns. This is a strong indicator
that you do not want to be involved, even if
everything you say is positive. Your verbal
message can be overruled by your body
message.

Think: 'What is the message I give out to
others about *my availability to help?*'

YOUR EYES: 'I AM INTERESTED
IN WHAT YOU ARE SAYING'

We have already seen in Unit 2.3 that **eye
contact is vital** in maintaining and
communicating interest in what another
person is saying. Research shows that women
are usually more attentive than men in all
measures of gaze. Good gazing skills can give
you important information about when to stop
listening and start responding. Eye contact is
when you meet somebody else's eyes. You may
be perceived as bored or even tense if you
look down or away too often.

GROUP ACTIVITY 2 (5 MINS)

READING BODY LANGUAGE

**Try this short activity. You will need a
timekeeper.**

● **Get into pairs.**

● **Gaze into your partner's eyes for one
minute and communicate all you can
through your eyes alone.**

**This is not an easy activity. Do not be
surprised if you find it difficult. Eye
contact can be a very intimate thing but
it is useful to explore our own responses**

to it. How did the exercise feel? How has it affected the relationship between you and your partner? Discuss these things between yourselves.

YOUR FACE: 'I AM FOLLOWING YOU CAREFULLY'

Your face is an obvious source of a great deal of information to anyone speaking to you. Anger, disgust, interest, surprise, fear, happiness and contempt are all expressions which can readily be registered facially. Someone who shows an expression which is relaxed and smiling usually demonstrates interest. But the counsellor has the added task of trying to convey to clients the message that their emotions are being understood. So, for example, when a client tells you that s/he is in the throes of coping with a major bereavement your face can respond to this by showing genuine concern at the bad news.

YOUR GESTURES: 'I AM INTERESTED'

What **habitual gestures** do you make? Maybe your friends can tell you. There is an activity which invites this kind of comment later on in this unit because it is so important for you to have information about how you come across to other people. The following is a list of gestures which are unhelpful in the counselling situation:

☹ fiddling with your hair;

☹ tightly clenching your hands;

☹ scratching yourself;

☹ clearing your throat frequently;

☹ firmly crossing your arms in front of you (this creates a barrier);

☹ pinching your ear;

☹ cleaning or fiddling with your glasses;

☹ putting your hand over your mouth;

☹ a fixed smile.

Are you aware of any such gestures in your own behaviour?

One of the most helpful gestures in counselling is the short nod of the head. This can be viewed as a reward to the client of your own agreement, reception of the message, or interest. It is important to note here that selective nodding can be negative because if you only nod at things which you yourself agree with, you can control certain clients. They will quickly learn to say the 'right' things in order to gain your approval.

YOUR CLOTHES: 'I AM AN APPROPRIATE PERSON FOR YOU TO RELATE TO'

Your clothes say a lot about you. The messages they give can relate to your self-esteem, your occupation, your sexuality, your confidence socially, your ethnicity, how much you conform to peer groups, your individuality and so forth. A successful accountant who is highly stressed will probably respond better to formal rather than to very informal dress. Your clothes, your hair, your cleanliness, your neatness/tidiness all send out messages about you and show how well you take care of yourself.

RULES IN BODY LANGUAGE

Everyone has her/his own personal 'rules' for **appropriate body language**. These can of course vary enormously from individual to individual. Often a person's rules reflect his or her cultural background; for example, Latin American people stand very close to each other by British standards. But not everyone's rules are culturally bound and nowadays many cultures are in a state of flux. For example, who would have thought in the 1950s that topless sunbathing would be acceptable in public for many British people? Even now British culture contains a variety of views on this issue: some sunbathe topless and some do not; those who do not may approve or disapprove when others do so.

' It is important to know and understand the rules that work best for your client. S/he will need to feel comfortable if s/he is to disclose something of her/his inner self to you. Learn to judge the space needed, the body language that s/he responds to, whether s/he likes to be touched or physically welcomed in some way or not.

SENDING EFFECTIVE VOICE MESSAGES

The **quality of your voice** can enhance the emotional tone of a conversation. When I supervise trainee teachers in the classroom I pay particular attention to how they use their voice to communicate with pupils. Two of the most common faults are to speak too quickly or too quietly. Both of these can indicate anxiety or nervousness. Your voice speaks volumes! It is the most obvious indicator of how you are feeling. Think for a minute what is involved when you speak verbally.

PITCH

This is the **highness or lowness of your voice.** Errors of pitch can be too high or too low. Some people heighten or lower their pitch if they are nervous. A pleasing voice without strain is easy for the majority of people to listen to.

VOLUME

How **loud or how quiet** is your voice? Does your voice fade away at the end of your sentences? Does the volume of your voice alter when you are in the counselling role? If you counsel in a loud voice it may come across as domineering; if you counsel in a quiet voice it may come across as weakness. Ask other people how they perceive the volume of your normal speaking voice.

PACE

This is the **rapidity with which you speak.** There are many factors involved in pace:

- words per minute;
- frequency and duration of pauses between words or sentences;
- use of silences;
- shortness of sentence construction.

A counsellor who speaks rapidly may contribute to a client's anxiety rather than calming her/him. A counsellor who speaks too slowly may indicate to the client that s/he is bored or that s/he is disinterested.

ARTICULATION

This refers to **the clarity of your speech** and whether your words are pronounced clearly. If you have nasal or guttural tendencies in your speech you may need some help from professionals before you can begin to help others. Regional accents are all right *in situ* but in another part of the country they can obscure the clarity of the messages you want to give.

PERSONAL REFLECTION

Look at the list below and mark whether you prefer, do not mind or positively dislike each type of behaviour. Record in writing your own results. You might like to pair up with another person and to discuss the similarities and differences between you. Or you might use the list for gaining personal understanding of how you evaluate other people.

☺ **A strong, firm handshake.**

☺ **A weak handshake which just touches you.**

☺ **Someone you meet for the second or third time giving you an embrace.**

☹ **Someone looking directly into your eyes when you are conversing.**

☺ A new acquaintance who stands at a proximity of between 12 and 15 inches to yourself.

☺ A person smoking without asking your permission.

☺ Someone in conversation with you who is preoccupied by a button, by her/his fingernails or by fiddling with her/his hair/rings/jewellery.

☺ Low-cut dresses and short skirts on women.

☺ Men with long hair and/or beards.

☺ Somebody looking elsewhere when s/he is talking to you.

SELF-EVALUATION/GROUP ACTIVITY 3

HEIGHTENING AWARENESS
OF HOW YOU COME ACROSS

This activity has two purposes. If it is done well by everybody it can give a very good indication of how you come across in a discussion situation. It also heightens powers of observation and gives an opportunity to view a range of behaviours and responses at the same time. The exercise is even more accurate if one of you can video record part of the group interaction.

● Form a group, ideally of three pairs of people: pair 1, pair 2 and pair 3. If this is not possible, two groups of two people will also work. Each pair is divided into A and B.

● Each pair has five minutes during which A argues a case chosen from the list below. It is best if you choose to argue for an opinion that you actually disagree with; see if you can find one. B is to take the alternative stance.

● Join with the other two pair(s) who have been doing the same thing. Each pair in turn are to sit face-to-face and argue opposite ends of the case they have chosen. They do this for five minutes. Whilst they are doing this the remaining two pairs sit sideways on and record their observations in three categories: what they have *seen*, *heard* and *felt*. Observers should distinguish carefully between the categories. You might like to write down your impressions in columns. Try to avoid confusion between good observation (with evidence) and your own personal opinion.

THEMES

☺ I should not have to compliment others. They should know how I feel from the way I act. Besides, I feel funny complimenting them.

☺ Why should I compliment someone who is getting paid to do the job?

☺ If I go around complimenting people and telling them how much I appreciate them, they will think I want something from them.

☺ People just think you are insincere if you pay them a compliment.

☺ I do not pay compliments because people just do not know how to take them; they get all flustered or embarrassed.

☺ If someone says something nice about me then I have to say something nice back.

☺ Other people enjoy hearing sincere, positive expressions of the way you feel about them.

☺ Expressing a compliment almost always deepens and strengthens a relationship.

☺ When people are complimented, it is less likely that they will feel unappreciated or taken for granted.

GROUP FEEDBACK

Everyone gets together for a final discussion. Give some time to the subject matter (giving compliments), some to issues of habitual behaviour and some to the effectiveness of the task-oriented group.

Personal Diary

THE ART OF CREATIVE CONFRONTATION

What does the word 'confrontation' conjure up in your thinking? An angry conversation? An aggressive interchange? An insistence from one person that the other does what s/he wants? In this unit we are not talking about confrontation along those lines at all. Confrontations used in the counselling situation are **interactions between counsellor and client which challenge the client's existing perceptions of her/himself**: for example, blind spots, distortions of reality, inconsistencies in her/his own thinking and so on. At one time or another when you are counselling a client you will have to confront her/him creatively to change her/his perspective, or the way s/he thinks about her/himself.

You may have already experienced confrontation from a good friend who loves and respects you. This is the best sort of confrontation because it comes from someone who supports you but who has the courage to disagree with your point of view. Such a friend is precious indeed, as the writer of Proverbs says: *'The kisses of an enemy may be profuse, but faithful are the wounds of a friend'* (Proverbs 27:6).

✔ AIMS

The aims of this unit are:

● To explore the language of creative confrontation.

● To look at confrontation at various levels of behaviour.

● To give you models of effective confrontation.

● To practise confronting someone in the counselling situation.

STARTER ACTIVITY (10–15 MINS)

EXPLORING YOUR OWN RESPONSES TO CONFRONTATION

Below are three different incidents in which the possibility of confrontation arises. What comes closest to how you would respond? Mark your own responses and then discuss your own feelings regarding confrontations of this sort.

1. **You are on holiday. An attractive restaurant advertises itself as 'the best food in the South West' and accolades from customers are on display in the foyer. You decide to eat there. To your amazement the food that you are served is half-cooked, and the portions are insufficient and cold. Do you:**

   (a) Not say anything for fear of embarrassment and hassle, but never go there again?

   (b) Leave the food as an indication of your discontent and write to the manager when you have left?

   (c) Confront the situation and ask to have a word with the manager there and then?

2. **You are going through a very stressed time at work; the workload is increasing and your boss expects you to do the impossible. You want to leave the job because your**

unhappiness is so great but you decide to talk it over with your partner/girlfriend/boyfriend/close friend. S/he just tells you that it is your own fault and that if you organized your life better you would be able to cope. You are hurt by her/his lack of understanding. Would you be more likely to:

(a) Feel hurt but say nothing for fear of causing more hurt?

(b) Wait until a future time to talk about the issue again and find out the reasons why your partner/friend thought this way?

(c) Confront the issue there and then and say that you were disappointed and hurt that s/he blamed you for your own stress, and that it has affected the relationship you have with her/him?

3. You find out that the local clergy have been talking about you and that they have misunderstood your intentions rather badly. Would you be more likely to:

(a) Not say anything, but pray about it?

(b) Talk to a trusted friend and ask for their advice about what to do?

(c) Make an appointment with the vicar to talk about the issue and to confront these misunderstandings?

A score of all or mostly (a)s indicates a passive response; a score of all or mostly (b)s indicates a delaying response; and a score of all or mostly (c)s indicates an assertive response.

GROUP FEEDBACK
What did people score and would they like to be different?

CONFRONTING DISTORTIONS OF REALITY

The way a person perceives her/himself can be a **distortion of reality**. It is not unusual in the counselling situation to find clients saying things such as:

☹ 'Nobody bothers whether I live or die.'

☹ 'I am no good at relationships—they all fail.'

☹ 'He just likes dangling me on a string.'

Clients' perceptions will have varying degrees of accuracy. Counsellors can either challenge what they consider to be false notions of reality or they can assist the clients to assess their own reality. One well-known way of mismanaging reality is to polarize everything in life into black/white, good/bad, right/wrong: for example, 'I am the best/absolute worst in the group' or 'I am the most popular/nobody can stand me'.

Unless people are very stuck in neurotic behaviour they will usually respond to some form of logical thinking. You can often help them by saying something like: 'I know you say... but show me what evidence you have for believing this.' Below you will find several sentences which can be used to confront misperceptions gently. Use them in the group activity on page 121.

● 'What has led you to this conclusion?'

● 'What you've said there doesn't make sense of what you told me yesterday.'

● 'Is there another way of looking at that?'

● 'What would you like to happen instead— what can you do about this?'

● 'How can you be so certain?'

GROUP ACTIVITY 1 (15–20 MINS)

LEARNING CONFRONTATION

● Get into pairs and label yourselves A and B. A is the counsellor; B is the client. You will need a clean sheet of paper and two pens. Rearrange your chairs/seating so that you are back-to-back.

● B starts the exercise by copying this statement down:

'I have come to you because I am an utter failure. I see my friends happily married and making a success of their lives and here I am—separated from my wife/husband, disliked by almost everybody and with little to look forward to.'

● Now B passes the paper over her/his back without speaking to A, who writes down what s/he would say to open up the issues. The paper then passes back and forth and the written conversation continues as both A and B give their own responses. As the conversation develops A should practise confronting fixed perceptions of self.

GROUP FEEDBACK

After fifteen to twenty minutes, each pair has a script which is then read to the wider group. Feed in your ideas for everyone's information.

CONFRONTING POWERLESSNESS

Powerlessness is a condition that people experience when they **fail to acknowledge the choices that they have**. It is a very common root of depression, but for the most part untrue. Everyone has choices. Even when our circumstances will not budge we have choices about how to respond. When our bodies fail us, or when we contract even terminal illness, we have some choice in how we live in the light of this. Our choices may be limited but it is difficult to imagine a situation where there is no choice at all.

This book is all about equipping people, whether counsellors or not, with a fuller range of life skills so that we have increased personal choice about the way we live, behave and act. Of course personal choice also means personal responsibility. There are many situations in which people avoid personal responsibility in the events of life. This often happens when they feel that it is someone else's fault that they are suffering, or that there are external factors which are immovable. It can also occur when something conclusive happens, for example when a close friend or relation dies and the event is irreversible. However, even in situations as painful as bereavement, sooner or later there are choices available to the person who is left behind.

Below are some guidelines to help you consider how to challenge other people in the fixed perceptions which contribute to their lack of well-being.

GUIDELINES FOR CONFRONTING AND CHALLENGING POWERLESSNESS

ATTEND ACCURATELY

As a starting-point, it is always important to let the client know that **you have both heard and understood him or her with a fair degree of accuracy**. This way s/he will feel that anything subsequent you say to him or her is earthed in a real appreciation of their predicament.

REFLECT INCONSISTENCIES

When you reflect the inconsistency of someone's view and then ask her/him to explain it you **open up the way for her/him to choose what s/he says and thinks**. For example, to a woman who is convinced that her husband does not love her you might say: 'Glenda, you say that he doesn't love you yet you also told me he went to a lot of trouble to decorate the house as you wanted it—how do you explain that?'

GAUGE THE AMOUNT OF ENERGY YOU PUT INTO THE CONFRONTATION

The power with which you confront anyone is sometimes referred to as **'muscle'**. Learn to gauge power according to the situation. Strong confrontation can be very useful at certain times but it can also cause resistance, especially if you are in the early stages of the counselling process and the client does not know you well.

WATCH YOUR BODY LANGUAGE

If you are tense about having to confront or you find it awkward you may find that your voice becomes higher or that you clench your hands. Avoid this; it can seem quite threatening.

THE CLIENT DETERMINES THE USEFULNESS OF CONFRONTATION

Ask the client whether the times when you have challenged her/him have moved her/him forward or not. Perhaps some have and some have not. **Learn to discern which types of confrontation are most helpful to which person.** Often your challenges will be slight; no big deal, just a common way of handling the material which is presented to you. If this is well-timed and well-worded it is unlikely to cause defensiveness. Make sure you do not overdo it, though—none of us likes to be challenged all the time.

GROUP ACTIVITY 2 (15 MINS)

CONFRONTATION IN COUNSELLING

With the above guidelines in mind, this exercise is designed to get you to work out two or three ways in which you would confront the self-defeating perceptions illustrated in the scenarios below.

- **Get into pairs to do a role-play. Choose one of the brief scenarios below. One of you takes the part of the client and the other takes the role of the counsellor. Enact a possible counselling session in which the client tries to maintain her/his fixed view and the counsellor uses the skill of confrontation to challenge her/him. For those of you role-playing the client, if your counsellor does a good job of confronting you, make sure you change your responses to suit the situation. You are not here to be belligerent!**

- **Remember to de-role when you finish. The group leader should allow a minute or two for you to 'resume' being who you really are. You can do this using a little ritual where you turn to your partner and say 'I am [name]' and s/he turns to you and says 'I am [name]'. Discuss the role-play between you and assess its development and value.**

SCENARIOS

- **Angela, aged forty-five, who says, 'I hate to have to visit my mother three times a week, but there's no one else to look after her.'**

- **Gerald, aged sixty-two, whose wife died two years ago: 'There's nothing for me now, I'm all on my own, I never go out, I just sit all day and remember.'**

REFRAMING: CREATIVE CONFRONTATION

Have you ever noticed how different you can look if you wear a certain colour? You are the same person but the colour has made all the difference. The same happens when you take an old painting in to have it reframed. With the right frame it can look stunning. With the wrong frame it has nothing going for it. It is the same picture, but the reframing makes all the difference.

The same word, **'reframing'**, applies to a particular skill in the field of counselling. Reframing is what a skilful counsellor does when s/he changes the way a client perceives a fixed situation. S/he 'reframes' the picture that the client has. For instance, it is well known that when relationships decline it is often because partners see each other in very negative frames. Consider the situations described below and then follow how the clients reframed them with the counsellor's help. In every case this helped the client to look deeper into the dynamics of (a) her/his own perceptions and (b) the life situation of those they were casting in a negative light.

☹ NEGATIVE FRAME: 'THEY'RE LAZY AND IT'S UNFAIR'

Jed, aged twenty-eight, was a cleaner at a small factory. He was busy all day doing hard manual labour but he did not perceive any of the other staff as doing any real work: all they did was carry paper, answer the phone and do checklists of goods arriving—and they were better paid. His anger grew and grew, and finally his work attitude suffered so much that his line manager suggested a visit to the counsellor. The company counsellor helped him to acknowledge his own anger and frustration, but offered the reframe that these 'white collar workers' were also working. They too were stressed because although they did not sweat all day, they often worked long hours to sort out problems. They also suffered mental fatigue because they were dealing with written and contractual material all day.

Jed refused this reframe. But he found out for himself how hard they really worked after he left the company, unable to resolve his discontent, and started off in his own cleaning business on a government enterprise scheme. The administration caused him more stress than the work!

In this example, the perception of the 'workers who are lazy and yet get better pay' is reframed as the 'workers who also work hard but with their heads not their hands'. The issue of pay was a separate one, though also important, and should have been discussed with his line manager.

☹ NEGATIVE FRAME: 'HE'S SO SELFISH', 'SHE'S ALWAYS NAGGING'

Tim and Laura found that their relationship had deteriorated to such a degree that they agreed to go for counselling. Tim perceived Laura as disliking him rather than loving him because she was always nagging him. Laura perceived Tim as being totally selfish because he arrived home late at night, never helped in the house or with the kids, and they never had quality time together. The counsellor acknowledged the anger, disappointment and frustration that existed for both of them and offered both Tim and Laura reframes:

- Tim was offered the reframe that Laura was a tired parent who had to do all the household chores, childminding and part-time work single handed. When she became overtired she got irritable.

- Laura was offered the reframe that Tim was a working man who needed some 'space' between his hectic full-time commuter job and the rest of the evening.

Both Tim and Laura agreed to the counsellor's suggestion that they reframe their perceptions as these were self-defeating. When Tim returned home after work in the evening he would spend an hour on his own watching TV while Laura looked after the children and did the cooking. They would then have time together. At weekends Tim would do enough of the childminding and household chores for Laura to have time to herself.

The reframe in this example was effective because it did not take long for Tim and Laura's mutual gratitude to grow. Each felt that the other was making the effort to see that their individual needs were met.

Reframing does not necessarily solve a problem but it does tend to give space and time for more positive attitudes to grow. We do not grow in love or understanding, or in personal change and adjustment, if we are working in an atmosphere of blame and accusation. In such an atmosphere all we can do is try to survive by defending ourselves, by throwing back as good as we get or by spending all our energy creating bigger and better barriers so that we cannot be attacked.

The real power of reframing is that it interrupts the negative framing of a situation. However, this requires the cooperation of the person being counselled; the client must actually have some input and do the reframing her/himself. All the counsellor can do is offer an alternative frame. For example, in the case of Jed described above, the counsellor's attempt to reframe the situation resulted in no real benefit. He found out for himself later on when the stakes were much higher.

REFRAMING YOUR OWN PERCEPTIONS

It is possible to reframe your own fixed perceptions of self but this is usually a lot harder than helping someone else to do it. Nevertheless, as Joy in the case study below found out, it can be both necessary and helpful.

CASE STUDY: JOY

Joy was suffering from intense feelings of self-accusation. She was working flat out with little social time and even less with her family. Her work included university teaching, writing articles and books, supervising research students, and preparing numerous lectures and courses. Yet at her annual appraisal her professor told her that she was not doing enough in producing research articles. She experienced an intense sense of failure that would not go away. It began to erode her sense of self-esteem. She felt that she had been judged and found wanting. She was discouraged. Then a good friend, Miriam, popped in for a coffee and asked how things were. It all came out—the sense of utter failure and inability to fit in all her workload. 'Oh,' said Miriam, 'that's not how I see it at all. From what you've told me your students are all well catered for and contented—you are writing books and preparing well for all sorts of new courses as well as everything else. No, I would disagree with your sense of failure. I'd say it's more a case of a highly successful professional woman who tries to please too much and reach perfection. Joy, something will have to go.'

In this situation Miriam was no professional counsellor but she had actually offered her friend a reframe for how she saw herself. In fact, Joy did not agree with her friend but it got her thinking and that meant that her fixed perceptions were being challenged. She went on to reframe for herself quite successfully.

PERSONAL REFLECTION

Think of a relationship you have had or have at the moment which needs some reframing. Practise the skill of suspending your own opinion/judgment for a short while and set about doing a reframe of the perceptions you have fixed for yourself about this person.

SELF-EVALUATION

What was hardest about the personal reflection exercise above? Can you reframe your fixed ideas of yourself? Choose a negative situation or perception that you have about yourself. See if you can reframe it in a different way. Evaluate whether there are any other ways of seeing the situation you are in.

Personal Diary

5.3 THE SKILL OF SELF-DISCLOSURE

One of the most important ingredients of any real friendship is the ability to disclose something of who you are—your opinions, thoughts, feelings, hopes, disappointments, aspirations. There is strong evidence to suggest that effective counsellors are also high on self-disclosure. They are not afraid to talk about themselves, particularly to reveal what they are thinking and feeling in an interaction as it occurs, that is, in the present tense.

This unit concentrates on the how, when and what of self-disclosure in the counselling role.

✔ AIMS

In this we have the following aims:

- To explore different forms of self-disclosure.

- To help you to evaluate your own habitual behaviour in terms of sharing with others about yourself.

- To identify skills and abilities that support effective self-disclosure in the counselling situation.

STARTER ACTIVITY (30 MINS)

SYMBOLS OF MYSELF

Symbols can represent thoughts, ideas and wishes or they can represent people. For example:

☺ Lionheart = King Richard.

☺ The lamb, the vine, the light of the world, the bread of life = Jesus.

This activity is designed to give you the opportunity to be self-disclosing in a structured exercise which focuses on symbols for various aspects of your life.

- Elect a leader who also keeps time for the group: five minutes should be allowed for each section (twenty minutes) in all and five minutes for the discussion to complete the exercise. Everyone should have a clean sheet of paper, some coloured felt-tips or crayons, a pencil and rubber.

- Individually, draw a shield similar to the one in the diagram below and divide it equally into four. There should be space for a personal motto underneath.

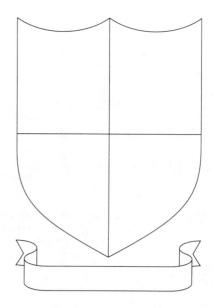

- In the top left-hand corner write 'My symbol' and draw anything which represents yourself. Although you cannot use words, you are not expected to be an artist.

- In the top left-hand corner draw a symbol for what you hope for yourself in ten years' time.

- In the bottom right-hand corner draw a symbol that represents your spiritual self or your spiritual self at the moment.

- In the bottom right-hand corner draw a symbol that somehow represents the friendships you possess at this time in your life.

- In the space at the bottom try to design a motto that in some way sums up one aspect of your character, for example, 'A man of many thoughts', 'She lives to help others'.

GROUP FEEDBACK

When you have completed part or all of the exercise in the time given, join with three or four other people. Each person has two to three minutes in which to select one or more of the items in the shield and talk about it. If the group has time you might like to discuss how that exercise felt and how easy or difficult it was to share with others.

(Adapted from an exercise in the book *New Methods in Religious Education Teaching* by Hammond, John *et al.*)

SELF-DISCLOSURE: GETTING THE MEASURE RIGHT

It is common sense that the skilled helper has to **find a happy medium between revealing too little and revealing too much**. To reveal too much early on in a relationship is not wise. It has been known for counsellors to dive straight into descriptions of their own problems, which prolong focus on the helper instead of the client. A useful distinction is to examine the difference between self-expressive and self-disclosing responses.

SELF-EXPRESSIVE RESPONSES

These are **immediate expressions of the counsellor's feeling about what the client has just said and done.** In other words you show as a counsellor that you are involved in the conversation. Personal expressions from the counsellor show that the counsellor has a personal involvement in what is being said and, if this is genuine, the client feels s/he is relating to a real person and not just to someone in the counselling role. Here are three types of self-expressive comments:

- **Comments on what the client has disclosed:** these include 'I'm so sorry to hear that', 'I am very pleased for you' or 'I'm excited about that'.

- **Comments on the clients themselves as people:** positive personal comments such as 'I admire your determination', 'I applaud your tenacity' or 'You have a delightful sense of humour'.

- **Comments on the counselling relationship:** these include 'I'm not so sure about what you have just said, it doesn't fit in somehow', 'I'm pleased with the tenacity that you are showing' or 'I'm worried because I sense that you see me in the same light as your mother'.

SELF-DISCLOSING RESPONSES

Self-disclosure on behalf of the counsellor may take many forms. The following examples are a small sample of different forms of self-disclosure that could be useful if treated sensitively:

- **The counsellor may reveal that s/he has had similar experiences herself.** This may help to reasssure the client that s/he is not the only one who is going through this particular experience. (Remember it is not helpful to assume that the client's experience is identical to your own.)

- **The counsellor may give some feedback to the client about how s/he perceives her/him.** This is best done at the request of the client her/himself and it should be stressed that it is only the counsellor's opinion. Why this sort of caution? Because feedback sessions recorded from counsellors show that often there are aspects of the counsellor's own projections or prejudice involved in such comments.

- **The counsellor may choose to share her/his problems with the ongoing counselling relationship.** S/he might admit to confusion or frustration—this demonstrates that s/he is human. It is also possible that s/he would suggest that the counselling is not producing any tangible good and that therefore it should be terminated.

- **The counsellor expresses something about her/his own experience of the client's situation.** To be effective, of course, this has to ring true for the client.

GROUP ACTIVITY 1 (15 MINS)

SELF-DISCLOSURE IN COUNSELLING

- **Join with one or two other people.**

- **Your task is to write two lists. The first is appropriate self-disclosure for the counsellor to offer a client. The second is inappropriate self-disclosure.**

- **What is the difference between the two? What makes self-disclosure inappropriate or unhelpful? Have you ever been on the receiving end of unhelpful self-disclosure?**

- **Discuss in your groups whether there are different perceptions between men and women on this issue.**

GROUP FEEDBACK

The course coordinator may ask each group for brief feedback on their main points.

THE JOHARI WINDOW

One of the most quoted models of self-disclosure is the Johari window which is illustrated in the modified diagram on page 129.

- **The open self:** what can be seen by everybody and involves parts of yourself that you understand and are happy to let others see.

- **The secret self:** usually involves a large part of the stream of consciousness which includes thoughts and fantasies. A person may have sexual fantasies about the people s/he meets or s/he may have fantasies about what s/he would actually like to be, but cannot bring her/himself to reveal them. It may be appropriate not to reveal aspects of the secret self.

- **The unaware self:** involves aspects of yourself which are clear to other people, but not to you. You might always laugh heartily when you are anxious or your throat may show tension. This is clearly visible to others but you have no personal awareness of it. In this counselling skills course, there have been exercises in which others have been given permission by you to comment on how they see you. Handled with care and love this can be a useful way of being more conscious of the unaware self.

Functions

	Known to Self	Unknown to Self
Known to Others	1 Open Self	2 Open Self
Unknown to Others	3 Secret Self	4 Unconcious Self

● **The unconscious self:** this is not available to anyone including yourself. It is quite possible that you could have strongly repressed feelings of anger, frustration, fear, or panic which are reflected in tense stomach muscles, a tightening in your jaw or clenched teeth. Unconscious feelings sometimes emerge during counselling training where there are learning structures which encourage exploration of feeling and experience. This can be very useful as it can give an insight into the unconscious self if you are willing to admit to the experience.

The Johari diagram can be altered in size and structure to indicate what your personal estimation of each category is/was. For example, you might say that before you started this course the *open self* was the smallest window, with the *unaware self* second smallest, the *secret self* second largest, and the *unconscious self* largest. The order may now have changed with the open self much bigger and the other windows altered too. Obviously the unaware self is the hardest to gauge! But when you get glimpses of insight or your unconscious self chooses to reveal itself in some way you could say that it has decreased.

PERSONAL REFLECTION

YOUR OWN JOHARI WINDOW

When you are on your own draw your own Johari window. Make the windows as large as you think each category merits at this time in your life experience. Write in what you can about the following:

● *Your open self:* what parts of you are open to the outside world.

● *Your unaware self:* comments others have made about aspects of yourself of which you have been unaware and which you may have doubted. If you cannot remember anything you may even want to ask good friends for some feedback.

● *Your secret self:* this activity is for your eyes only and for your own personal awareness. You may wish to symbolize your secret self, the part that only you know and do not wish to reveal to others. What does this say about you?

● *Your unconscious self:* this may just have to be left blank. But do think: has your unconscious ever given you a revelation or insight? Have you ever had feelings show involuntarily and wondered what on earth was going on?

This activity can be used in a number of ways:

☺ It may focus your self-awareness and expand it.

☺ It may give you food for thought.

☺ It may be that you realize there is work to do if you are to counsel and help others.

☺ It may lead you to pray through various areas of your life.

THE DECISION TO SELF-DISCLOSE

Counsellors will have a variety of decisions to make when they think about whether to make self-disclosures to the client. The first decision is almost always the decision of whether or not you should speak in this way at all. This involves a large degree of personal judgment about the usefulness of what you have to contribute and about what you know of the client. Expectations of clients differ across cultures, social class, race and gender, and those you seek to help will have their own idea of what is appropriate.

Second, you have to decide how honest to be in the situation and for this you have to know yourself well enough. For example, you may be going through your own emotional crisis; being a counsellor does not give you immunity! Imagine that your own marriage is in crisis and your client is in the same position. You must judge whether you have

sufficient detachment to disclose the experience you have had in a constructive manner. There is also the question of how the client receives what you have said. Look for her/his non-verbal communication and try to sense whether you can continue accordingly.

Third, disclosing facts is one thing but disclosing your personal feelings is another. Imagine that you have shared information about your own marital crisis; are you going to go on and share the depression, the sense of failure and so on that so often accompanies a situation like this?

Fourth, you will have to decide whether to talk about how you handled and coped with the situation; and last, you need to decide whether to conclude the episode and talk about how you feel now in the light of all this experience.

TRANSFERENCE AND COUNTER-TRANSFERENCE

Transference means what it says. It is about transferring something. In the field of counselling this term usually refers to clients transferring feelings they have for other people (for example, their mother, father, etc.) on to the counsellor. They are intentionally or unintentionally using the counsellor for their own emotional ends.

Counter-transference refers to negative and positive feelings that the counsellor transfers on to the client. Some counsellors use self-disclosure to manipulate clients to meet their own needs for approval, personal or even sexual intimacy. This can be both intentional and unintentional but it shows the importance of the need to be vigilant, to be aware of your own motivation and to behave ethically.

GROUP ACTIVITY 2 (15 MINS)

INTIMACY CIRCLES
This is an exercise designed to get you thinking about the different relationships

in your life. Every member of the group should have a piece of paper and pencil.

● First, each group member working on her/his own, make a list of all the people—family, friends, colleagues and significant others—who are connected to you in some way.

● When you are satisfied with your list, draw a set of ever-widening circles as in the diagram below. In the centre put a dot which represents yourself. Now plot on the chart all of the people you have listed. You should plot them so that those you are the *most intimate* with come nearest to you on one of the lines of the circle. You will have to decide what you mean by close intimacy yourself; no one else can define it for you. (It is best to do this in pencil as you may discover that having plotted a number of people, you spot that someone you did not consider too intimate is actually on the same circle as someone you do.)

● Now look at the completed circle and ask yourself the following questions:

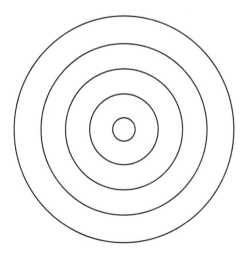

■ Is it accurate?

■ Is there anyone missing?

■ Does what you have done surprise you in any way? Have you plotted people differently than you expected? Is your unconscious self giving you information?

■ If you had done this a year/three/five years ago, would the diagram have looked different?

■ Is there any connection between those closest to you on the diagram and your own willingness to disclose your own feelings and thoughts with them? Or theirs with you? Or are other factors involved?

GROUP FEEDBACK

Discuss with one or two others in the group what changes you would like to appear on this chart. What needs to be done in order to effect change?

YOUR OWN LIFE EXPERIENCES: A RESOURCE BANK FOR EFFECTIVE SELF-DISCLOSURE

Your own life experiences are the raw material from which your counselling skills develop. Part of your sensitivity and the depth of your thinking will depend to some extent on the joys, trials, challenges and suffering that you have encountered thus far. Of course it is possible to have a variety of such experiences and to have learned very little about yourself. But the converse is also true: life can teach us many lessons and sometimes it does so the hard way. Take, for instance, someone who has suffered deep bereavement and the loss of somebody s/he loved deeply. Unless the feelings of grief and loss are all suppressed for a long period, s/he will experience some of the extremes of her/his own emotions. It is not uncommon to find that people in this situation are surprised at themselves. They discover unfamiliar parts of their inner self, the 'edges' of their personality that are sometimes unknown.

CASE STUDY: JOHN

John found that when his wife of twenty-eight years died he cried and sobbed for the first time in his life. But it went deeper than that. He could trace and remember the stages he went through in the grieving process. These changes were physical, psychological and spiritual. There was the loss to be acknowledged and felt and lived with. There was the anger to be accepted and expressed and worked on. There was his new single status and sense of self somehow to come to terms with. Issues of loss, anger and identity were just a few of the problems that John worked with over a period of years. None of these life events now make him a good counsellor but, because John is becoming a skilled helper, his own life provides him with a resource bank of authentic human experience. He has had to grow in response to this experience. He has had to journey in unknown psychological places, and he does not yet know who he is becoming. This has involved him in a process of personal development; in a sense he has walked the path that many of his clients will have to walk in the future. Their issues may be different ones to his own, but the process of change is the same. It takes us further. It sometimes means we are neither what we were nor what we are to become; there is disorientation and our identities may be in flux for an unknown period.

John understands this and he knows that he has grown through his own bereavement. He is a sensitive and skilled man and here is what he says about the usefulness of it all in the counselling work that he now does:

I don't pretend that my own loss and bereavement is directly helpful to my clients. Each client is their own individual person and there is nothing worse than a counsellor 'laying on you' their own sense of what is good for you, i.e. their own experience of life. But what I can offer in the light of the pain and suffering attached to losing my wife is my knowledge of the process of growth and change. I am much more able now to feel the extremes of emotion that some of my clients are experiencing. I know how fragile, forgetful, self-pitying, desperate, fraught, and insecure I myself got. I guess that my horizons on human experience have been painfully enlarged. I also know that things can change. After a life-crisis you are never the same again but, if you have the will to be, you are much more yourself than you have ever been before.

SELF-EVALUATION

What areas of your own life have been developed through change, crisis, bereavement or loss? On your own, at a time when you have the emotional energy and comfort to do this, think of the range of experience you have had. Write down what you think you have learned. What feelings have you discovered about yourself and others? Keep track of your own personal growth so that you have an aide-memoire. You may need it to help others.

Personal Diary

Module 6

SETTING COUNSELLING AND COMMUNICATION GOALS

6.1 SKILLS SURVEY
ASSESSING PERSONAL STRENGTHS AND WEAKNESSES

We have reached the last module in our course. The units in this part of the book are all about assessing our own personal strengths and weaknesses in the area of interpersonal relationships. It provides you with lists of skills which are fundamental to any good communication between people. You can then assess yourself. The module contains set situations from which you/your group can work on creating scripts and laying out possible solutions/strategies for effective communication. The secret of personal learning here is to be as honest as you can be both in identifying areas for your own improvement and in being comfortable with the areas you are well-skilled in. The British are notoriously embarrassed about complimenting themselves—please, if you deserve a top grade, give yourself one! In the interests of accurate assessment you have permission!

✔ AIMS

The aims of this unit are:

- To identify a wide range of skills which contribute to effective interpersonal communication.

- To assess your own strengths and weaknesses in communication skills.

- To give you the opportunity to create your own strategies for personal improvement.

STARTER ACTIVITY (10 MINS)

CONVERSATION SKILLS

Here are three skills that you need to make use of nearly every day in order to get along with other people. Read the description of each skill carefully and then give yourself the score which best describes how good you are at using it:

Score 1 if you are never good at it.

Score 2 if you are seldom good at it.

Score 3 if you are sometimes good at it.

Score 4 if you are often good at it.

Score 5 if you are always good at it.

You can score a maximum of 15 points for all three skills:

- *Starting a conversation:* talking to someone about light topics and then leading into more serious ones.

- *Continuing a conversation:* opening the main topic, elaborating on it and responding to the reactions of the person you are talking to.

- *Ending a conversation:* letting the other person know that you have been paying attention and then skilfully closing the conversation appropriately.

How did you do? Are you better at some of these than others?

GROUP FEEDBACK

Get into groups of between three and four people and compare your results. Then discuss between you some of the problems you meet in conversations you have with others.

HOW TO START CONVERSATIONS WITH OTHER PEOPLE

How do you start a conversation? Do you just start talking about what is on your mind at the time? Of course you don't. There are interesting unspoken 'rules' that accompany any start of a conversation and almost all starter topics for beginning conversations fall into the following groups:

- the environment/situation you are in;

- the news of the day/week;

- the person you are talking to;

- yourself.

THE ENVIRONMENT YOU ARE IN

Examples of this kind of beginning would be: 'It's so dark and humid today, isn't it?' or 'I don't know why these buses are always late, do you?' Statements such as these are acceptable to almost anybody and although nobody ever states this they are really giving the message 'I want to talk to you'. Most people can respond to these kinds of messages because they are non-threatening. They are not asking for thoughts or inner feelings, they are simply devices for starting you off on the road to conversation. If you scored low on starting conversations it is worth looking around you when you find yourself in a social gathering or at an occasion where you need to initiate conversation. Look and find something you can comment on: the decor, the garden, the amount of people there, the quality of the food, the nice wine and so on.

THE NEWS

This is always a safe bet unless you are trying to make a controversial political or moral statement of some kind. You can try comments such as: 'It looks like there's going to be another strike doesn't it?', 'Have you heard the cricket score?' or 'Do you know what's in the budget yet?' Most people can say something to openers like this—even if they do not know, it gives them the opportunity to ask you what you think.

THE PERSON YOU ARE TALKING TO

An example of this would be: 'I do like your coat, do you mind my asking where you bought it?' or 'That's a lovely leather bag, I can never find things like that when I'm looking for them'. Comments such as these are genuine compliments about what a person owns and, by adding something along the lines of '… I can never find anything like that' and so on, you give some information about yourself. If these comments are genuine, very few people fail to respond at some level because you have risked yourself in reaching out to them and because they are usually pleased that their good taste is shared by someone else.

YOURSELF

You may wish to start a conversation by saying, 'I play the guitar, but I don't get much practice these days' or 'I'm thinking of training as a counsellor, if I get the chance'. These are comments about yourself. They actually ask a lot more of the person you are talking to because s/he then has to respond to what you have said. S/he may not share the same interests but if you can match your own comments to something s/he obviously does have an interest in you are almost assured of a response. For example, talking about owning and loving pets—especially dogs and cats—is a great opener. Recently on holiday, I sat on a wall at St David's Cathedral in Wales watching a beautiful labrador wallow in the stream of water that flowed through the cathedral grounds. A married couple of similar age sat on the wall a little further along. They were enjoying the sight of the labrador as much as I was. I said: 'Labradors are lovely dogs, I think.' 'Yes,' they replied, 'we had one and we adored it.' From then on we were firmly established as holiday friends. Our communication starter was an obvious love of dogs. The love of gardens can be just as good an opener: 'Your roses are absolutely lovely.' What gardener is not going to respond with pleasure to this entry?

GROUP ACTIVITY 1 (15 MINS)

IMPROVING CONVERSATION
Get into groups of three or four people. If you are working individually you can also do this exercise just by yourself. One of you should record your work so that verbal feedback can be given to the wider group.

- **Pool the experiences of your group to see if there are any situations where you have felt awkward or challenged. Think of three situations in which people have to initiate conversation. List them.**

- **As a group devise at least three strategies, that is opening gambits, for conversation in each of these situations.**

GROUP FEEDBACK
Individual groups feed back their findings for wider discussion.

CONVERSATIONAL SKILLS TRAINING

Sometimes you find that the best form of counsel you can give someone is in the area of conversational skills training. Take, for example, the case of Mary.

CASE STUDY: MARY AND THE PROBLEMS OF BEING MARRIED TO A BISHOP

When Mary was a young woman of twenty-three she married David who was then training for the ministry. For years they worked together as a team in the parishes and in the communities in which they worked. Mary ran several women's groups and always supported David wholeheartedly in his work, but she would always avoid formal gatherings of clergy because she was shy and would dry up in conversation.

What she really dreaded was being placed next to strangers at formal dinners and being expected to make conversation. She was all right if she knew someone and it was better if she was seated next to a woman, but some of the male churchmen were very threatening.

When David was made a bishop her role became far more public and she continued to shy away from formal events. She did not want to let David down but the thought of all that tension and pressure contributed to her feeling ill before big events. The new job took its toll on David too and he needed the support and understanding of his wife more than ever. Their marriage began to suffer. Mary felt guilt at her own inadequacy and David felt let down. Then Mary took the initiative and asked for counselling.

She was clearly under stress about the present situation. She felt an utter failure and certainly not good enough for David. Clearly there were issues of self-esteem to be explored and after the counsellor had done some work with Mary on this she addressed the issue of public meetings.

Mary: I can't do it. I just feel sick at the thought of it.

Counsellor: What goes through your head when you imagine the event?

Mary: Well, I imagine myself sandwiched between two erudite bishops or senior clergy, and

I am dreading them talking to me in case I make a fool of myself.

Counsellor: *I'd like to offer you my thoughts on this, Mary. From what you've told me, there is a sense of real panic which takes over—am I right?*

Mary: *Absolutely—that's just how it is.*

Counsellor: *And then you feel as if things are out of your control—anything could happen. You feel utterly powerless.*

Mary: *Yes, it's as if I am just waiting for the worst and I can't do anything.*

Counsellor: *Well, Mary, what if you and I worked together on reducing that level of powerlessness and instead you trained yourself to have some control over events?*

Mary: *I'm willing, but I'm not sure how.*

Counsellor: *Well, instead of you waiting for the conversation to come to you when you dry up and feel awful, I am going to ask you to prepare yourself for conversation. I want you to do your homework. Go home and, when you are on your own, research three topics you can choose from to initiate conversation. Make one of them a personal issue that you are interested in, one of them a church issue that is topical and one of them something that is in the news at the moment. Then practise each category in the following way: (a) ask a question to the other person (b) state a fact to her/him (c) voice your own opinion. When you've done this practise all of your openers. You have choices you can make now, according to whom you are speaking to. Then come back next week and we will do some role-play.*

The skills training made all the difference for Mary. From then on she had a strategy that gave her a measure of control over her circumstances. Years later she was still preparing; she would write down her homework before important social gatherings. Mary never gained the sort of confidence she would have liked but she managed to do what she wanted to well.

GROUP ACTIVITY 2 (15 MINS)

SKILLS SURVEY

Throughout this course you have had the opportunity to practise and improve a number of counselling and communication skills. Below you will find a comprehensive list of skills, including some covered in this course. Look again at the marking scheme for the starter activity in this unit and individually spend about fifteen minutes going down the list and giving yourself a score (out of five) for your competence in each skill at this moment in time:

☺ *Listening:* **paying attention to people, trying to understand them and letting them know you are trying.**

☺ *Expressing a compliment:* **telling someone that you like something about her/him or about her/his actions.**

☺ *Asking for help:* **requesting that someone help you in handling a difficult situation which you have not been able to manage by yourself.**

☺ *Expressing affection:* **letting someone know that you care about her/him.**

☺ *Responding to the feelings of others:* **trying to understand what other people are feeling and communicating your own understanding to them.**

☺ *Delaying gratification:* **suspending your own need for pleasure/ assurance/confirmation until a more appropriate time.**

☺ *Persuading others:* **attempting to convince another person that your** ideas are better and will be more useful than her/his.

☺ *Suspending judgment:* holding your views/analysis of a situation lightly until you have more information and facts to go on.

☺ *Responding to praise:* letting a person know that you are pleased with her/his praise and that you appreciate it.

☺ *Responding to failure:* thinking out what went wrong and what you can do about it so that you can be more successful in the future.

☺ *Apologizing:* telling someone that you are sorry for something you have done.

☺ *Responding to contradictory messages:* recognizing and dealing with the confusion that results when a person tells you one thing but speaks or behaves as if s/he means something else.

☺ *Setting priorities:* deciding which problem is more urgent than the rest and should be tackled first.

☺ *Self-control:* controlling what you do and say before things get out of hand.

☺ *Determining responsibility:* finding out whether your actions or the actions of others have caused something to happen.

☺ *Preparing for a stressful conversation:* planning ahead of time to present your plans/point of view in a conversation which promises to be strained.

☺ *Gathering information:* deciding what specific information you need, finding out what place or what person can help you in the process.

☺ *Setting goals and strategies:* deciding on what you want to accomplish and anticipating whether your plan is likely to succeed or not.

☺ *Responding to persuasion:* carefully considering what another person says and weighing their point of view against your own before deciding what action to take.

☺ *Taking risks:* being aware that actions and behaviours which are tried and tested are not able to solve a problem/situation, and deciding to try something which is not personally familiar.

Now look at the scores you have given yourself in this exercise. With a partner define any common features between your two sets of scores: for example, skills you have both marked high or low. Establish between you a priority list of three issues which you want to work on together to improve. Now work on one or more of these according to the chart on implementing self-directed change in the self-evaluation section below.

SELF-EVALUATION: IMPLEMENTING SELF-DIRECTED CHANGE

● Determine three skills or abilities which you want to be able to do or achieve a level of proficiency in. Define each goal clearly: 'I want to be able to do... especially when...'

● Identify as many skills/ways of behaving which are connected with your goals as you can.

● List the people, places and times where you could possibly practise some of these skills. Try to choose venues which are relatively secure and less threatening to start off with.

● Order the list so that you now have a sequence from the most difficult to the easiest objective you are going to attempt.

● Set a reasonable 'first guess' time by which you will have carried out the first and easiest step on your line. Then do the same for the second step and so on. Determine how many times you intend to practise each step.

● You only learn skills by practice. You are going to have to work hard. Carefully pick your way through your list one item at a time.

● Set a time with your partner when you are going to meet and have a mutual review of how you are getting on and what you are achieving. Are your steps too big? Are they unrealistic? Do you need to change anything? Should you write a new list or get help?

● When you have achieved a goal, give yourself some kind of reward and go on to the next thing.

PERSONAL REFLECTION

Keep a journal record of all your feelings and thoughts associated with working on gaining the skills you identified in the self-evaluation exercise above. If you are determined and tenacious you will find that there is improvement. Christians also have the resource of prayer. Your journal can be a disciplined way of keeping track of your own personal development. Your spiritual task will then be to ask God for help and persistence, and insight into how to bring about the changes that will make you a more effective helper and servant for him. It is also a great

strength to have a prayer partner/co-counsellor who is as concerned as you about this area of personal growth.

Personal Diary

THE SKILLS OF SELF-CONFIDENCE AND ASSERTION

Misunderstandings arise every day. Many of these are never resolved because the people involved are not assertive enough to be direct and honest, or to check out what is happening at the time that it occurs.

If we are to function effectively for God, ourselves, our families and the wider community there are times when we will have to assert ourselves:

- Imagine that your family times together are being eroded by lots of long phone calls from friends who need information or help. You need to set some boundaries with them. This means asserting yourself.

- Imagine that your young son or daughter is the victim of bullying at school and after repeated efforts on your behalf nothing has been done. A different level of assertion is needed.

- Imagine that your husband/wife repeatedly causes you extreme stress and concern. You need sensitive skills of assertion to voice your own hurt, disappointment and anger.

Self-assertion comes naturally to some people but has to be learned by the vast majority of us. Assertion is not to be confused with aggression. It is not trying to force people to do what you want them to do, as we will see from the examples we give in this unit.

Many people come for counselling and are helped by it but lack the skills to maintain a level of emotional health because they are non-assertive in protecting and affecting the things that matter to them. The assertive issues which are explored in this unit are of use to everyone; they are important life skills that most of us never learned in school.

✔ AIMS

The aims of this unit are:

- To distinguish between passive, assertive and aggressive behaviour.

- To help you think through and evaluate your own views of and assumptions about assertive behaviour.

- To identify areas of self-assertion which are important for your own development.

- To teach assertive skills to enable people to set appropriate limits, that is, learning to say no.

THE DIFFERENCE BETWEEN ASSERTION AND AGGRESSION

Assertion is frequently mistaken for aggression. For example, the assertive woman can be perceived as someone who is able to stand up for herself but who has lost her warmth, compassion and sensitivity. Many women, in trying to steer as far as possible from being aggressive, repress legitimate feelings and expressions which could bring clarity and content to relationships. The same is often true for Christian men and women who believe that to be a Christian means never getting angry, negative or refusing to help others who need you.

Yet all of us at one time or another feel annoyed, resentful, frustrated or angry. All of us experience the physical side of these negative feelings. Blood pressure, increased heart rate, muscle tension and headaches can all be caused by negative feelings. A person essentially has three choices about the way s/he deals with negative feelings:

- We can inhibit our expression and say nothing or give 'hints' about how we are feeling by our behaviour or body language.

- We can accuse, attack or label the person we consider responsible and put her/him down.

- We can be honest and direct about how we feel at that moment.

Of course, people may use a mixture of all three. But there is usually a habitual way in which we handle different aspects of our lives: for example, a person may be aggressive at work but inhibited at home with intimate loved ones.

STARTER ACTIVITY (10–15 MINS)

PASSIVE, ASSERTIVE AND AGGRESSIVE BEHAVIOUR

Look at the situations in the box on page 145. Then get into groups of two or three and between yourselves, at an appropriate level for you, share with each other areas in which you feel you respond passively and/or assertively and/or aggressively. What happens when you are habitually passive in dealing with your negative feelings? Why do people prefer to be passive rather than assertive?

THREE BASIC LIFE POSITIONS: THE WORK OF THOMAS HARRIS

In his book *I'm OK. You're OK* (1973) Thomas Harris provides a framework to show the attitudes underlying the three responses of assertiveness, aggression and passivity. These are summarized as:

- Assertiveness: I'm OK—You're OK

- Aggression: 'I'm OK—You're not OK

- Passivity: 'I'm not OK—You're OK

The person who is assertive has the attitude:

'I'm OK and you are OK. I will show you my feelings and you have the same privilege. I will not allow you to take advantage of me and I hope you will do the same if I try to take advantage of you. I will not attack you for who you are.

I'm OK. You're OK.

The person who is aggressive has the attitude:

I'm OK, but you're not. Therefore, I will feel justified in criticising you and showing you what is wrong about you. Since you're not OK you deserve to be told.

I'm OK. You're OK.

The person who is generally passive frequently has an attitude which goes something like this:

You're OK, but I'm not. Therefore, I will be very careful of what I say. I'll try to make sure that I don't displease you, even if you do something that hurts me. There is so much wrong with me that I do not have the right to assert myself.

I'm OK. You're OK.

WHY BE ASSERTIVE?

Since being assertive requires a great deal of thought and effort why do people try to achieve it? In my own experience there are direct benefits when someone learns to be assertive. It helps us to avoid:

- misunderstandings;

- emotional withdrawal and behaviour that 'punishes' people, for example moods, rejection, distancing;

- hurting other people's feelings;

---

1. My husband/wife/partner/flatmate has not been helping me around the house. It is all up to me. We have guests for dinner one evening and as soon as they go home s/he slumps down in front of the television leaving me with all the dishes. I respond:

Passively: *by making a show of cleaning the dishes—banging pans together then going straight to bed without saying goodnight*

Assertively: *by saying, 'I don't want to clean up by myself. I would like you to do half'*

Aggressively: *Accusing her/him: 'You are so lazy. You only think about yourself and your own needs'*

2. I have been on the phone for over twenty minutes to a friend who is going on and on, and I have so many things to do before the evening is out. I respond:

Passively: *'I've got to go now, someone is at the door'*

Assertively: *'I am pushed for time as it's nearly 6 o'clock—let's continue another time'*

Aggressively: *'It's 6 o'clock, I have already been on the phone for twenty minutes, you should realize that'*

3. The minister calls and asks if I would be responsible for a weekly church group. I do not want to do this as I already have too many pressures. I respond:

Passively: *'Yes,' then slam down the phone and feel angry*

Assertively: *'I really don't want to take on that responsibility this year but I would like to consider it again next year'*

Aggressively: *'No, I already get asked to do too much—don't you realize the pressures of a normal working life?'*

4. My friend arranges to pick me up and take me to a day conference. S/he is forty minutes late. We have clearly missed the start of the meeting. I respond:

Passively: *by saying nothing, just a very vague 'hello' and there is an 'atmosphere' in the car as I am quiet with my own anger all the way to the conference*

Assertively: *'I am annoyed that you are forty minutes late. I don't like to miss the beginning of anything'*

Aggressively: *'You are so inconsiderate. You shouldn't make commitments you can't keep'*

- spending our time and energy unproductively by being angry, depressed or discouraged by something that has happened.

EXPRESSING NEGATIVE FEELINGS

Directly expressing negative feelings is difficult for many men and women. Anger, resentment and annoyance are often considered inappropriate emotions. When they first begin to assert themselves many people are concerned about the response they will get. The chances of negative responses are reduced if there is sensitive and careful assertiveness. Two things can help here:

- giving 'I' messages, not 'you' messages;

- pitching your level of intensity.

'I' AND 'YOU' MESSAGES

Dr Thomas Gordon, in his book *Parent Effectiveness Training*, urges parents to share their feelings with their children by way of 'I' messages rather than accusing them with 'you' messages. Examples of 'you' messages might be: 'You are very selfish', 'Stop it, you're so stupid to do that!'. Gordon encourages parents to say something like: 'I get angry when you make so much noise and interrupt everybody else, I want you to change things.'

This emphasis on the 'I' or 'you' message is important because it can change the whole dynamic that follows when negative feelings are being expressed. Take the following case study as an example.

CASE STUDY TAKE 1:
LIZ AND BARRY, THE 'YOU' MODEL

Liz and Barry have been married for just three months:

Liz: You were so rude last night. I hadn't even finished my meal when you suggested everyone leave for the theatre. You need to consider other people. (Liz accuses, reveals no personal feelings and lectures him.)

Barry: You always find something wrong with me. All you ever do is nag. There won't be a next time because I'm not going to mix with you and your friends together in public. (Barry responds as many children do by defending, counter attacking and then withdrawing.)

Liz and Barry have a difficult evening. A small incident has escalated into marital stress. Liz begins to question the value of sharing her feelings with Barry. And Barry tells himself that he will not be treated like a child. If Liz and Barry were to try again, this time assertively, there might be a difference.

CASE STUDY TAKE 2:
LIZ AND BARRY, THE 'I' MODEL

Liz: Barry, I was upset and embarrassed last night that you suggested leaving before I had even finished eating. I would like you to check
that I am ready before suggesting that we leave. (Liz states her feelings, does not attack Barry's character and takes responsibility for her own needs by telling him what she needs in future situations.)

Barry: 'I didn't realize, Liz, I was anxious to get to the show. I'll try to check with you next time but if I forget it's not intentional so just speak up and let me know. I won't mind. (Barry corrects any misunderstanding Liz has about his intentions, he shares his feelings with her, he acknowledges her request of him to change and he gives his own desire for Liz to express herself at the time.)

The probability that we will send a 'you' message when we are upset or angry is very high. So consistent practice and thought is needed to alter the habit. Even then, being assertive and expressing your own feelings rather than labelling someone else does not guarantee a favourable response.

GROUP ACTIVITY 1 (10–15 MINS)

HANDLING NEGATIVE FEELINGS

Here is a list of events which can cause negative feelings:

☹ **Asking strangers not to smoke in your presence or in your home.**

☹ **Discovering that you have been short-changed in a shop and asking for correct change.**

☹ **Disagreeing with your boss/course leader/about how you have been appraised in your work.**

☹ **Asking visitors to pay for their own phone calls.**

☹ **Telling a friend/partner that you disagree with her/his opinion.**

☹ **Being annoyed and angry because you are constantly interrupted.**

☹ Finishing a telephone conversation that has gone on for too long.

☹ Expressing love to someone who has not expressed it to you.

☹ Saying no to demands which put you under too much pressure.

☹ Expressing your feelings about being criticized or put down.

You can do this activity with a partner or by yourself.

● Look at this list and tick anything which you can identify as causing negative feelings for you.

● Select one issue to work on alone or with your partner. Consider what usually happens and how you normally react when this situation occurs.

● Rewrite a typical episode which shows how you have converted your response into an 'I' message.

● When you are ready, try out the new way of communicating and evaluate any difference in the way events develop.

GROUP FEEDBACK

The rewritten episodes can be read to the whole group.

PITCHING YOUR LEVEL OF INTENSITY

The degree of intensity you use in communicating your thoughts and feelings is an important concept to grasp. Some writers have called it 'muscle' power. You will feel uncomfortable with any assertion unless the level of muscle fits the intensity of the event.

In my work I train teachers, and often this is the hardest thing for them to learn. If a child is constantly kicking their chair the teacher may respond with:

● **Minus one, passivity:** a disapproving look, or ignoring the situation and hoping it will go away.

● **Muscle level one:** 'Would you please not kick the chair; you are distracting me from what I am saying.' Many children will respond at this level but others will not. If the intrusion persists the teacher moves to:

● **Muscle level two:** 'I don't want you to kick the chair again.' At this point not only are the words more forthright, but the tone, pitch, volume and facial expression should be more forceful. If there is no improvement then words need to be backed up with proposed action which is:

● **Muscle level three:** 'If you kick your chair again I am going to make a formal report on your bad behaviour.' At this level the teacher lets the child know the consequences of failing to comply.

● **Muscle level four:** the proposed action is carried out—the report is made and possible punishment is decided.

● **Plus one, aggression:** 'Get out of the class and stay out until you can behave yourself'.

Assertiveness can call for all levels of muscle. Moving from low to high levels means changing the verbal and non-verbal messages you give. 'I would like' is lower level than 'I want' or 'I must insist'. Assertion is most effective when the level of verbal and non-verbal muscle is just right for the different situations we meet. There are of course situations where progression in muscle power is not possible and the intensity of the event calls for instant high-level muscle. Equally it is sometimes right just to ignore something. But the hierarchy of levels proposed here is useful to enable us to look at the interim options available between the opposite poles of passivity and aggression.

PERSONAL REFLECTION

MUSCLE POWER

In this exercise you are invited to do your own personal thinking and work on an issue which is specific to you at this moment in time.

- Choose a situation in which you would like to be assertive instead of coping in your usual way. Clarify what it is you would like to be able to say and to whom.

- Using the muscle power levels described above, write out the different ways of communicating your message using verbal and non-verbal means.

- You can either leave the exercise at this point and pray and think further about it, or try out some of the different levels of communication the next time you meet the issue.

LEARNING TO SAY 'NO'

Setting limits shows other people the sort of person you are. When you set limits you give other people information about how you want to be treated. Counsellors find that setting limits is one of the most difficult areas of assertion for women because saying no to the requests and demands of others is seen as being impolite and unkind. Yet unless a person can protect her/his privacy and basic emotional needs for space and quality time with others, s/he is prone to depression and work overload.

GROUP ACTIVITY 2 (10–15 MINS)

SAYING NO

How do you rate on the learning to say no scale? Read the following situations and either say how you react or, if the situation is not directly relevant to you, imagine how you would react. Give yourself a score from 1 to 5:

1 = Always say no

2 = Sometimes say no

3 = Indecisive and cannot give an answer

4 = Hardly ever say no

5 = Never say no

- ☺ Your mother/father/grandparent phones you frequently and indicates that you should visit.

- ☺ A child demands your attention instantly.

- ☺ You are writing an essay/book/report which has deadlines and you get invites from good friends to go out.

- ☺ Friends call on the spur of the moment to see you.

- ☺ Your husband/wife/partner wants sexual loving when you do not feel like it.

- ☺ Answering the telephone.

- ☺ You are expected to attend the prayer meeting/Sunday service.

- ☺ People are going through real stress and need help.

- ☺ Add to this list if there is a specific concern that you wish to discuss.

Now join with two or three other people and look at those situations to which you gave the extreme score of 1 or 5. Discuss between yourselves:

● What do you gain and lose from this response?

● What do you fail to do because of the time spent on the things to which you never say no? Are there changes you would like to make?

SELF-EVALUATION

THOUGHTS THAT CAUSE PROBLEMS

In assertiveness training workshops, people have volunteered a number of thoughts that give them problems. These are listed below.

☹ Making mistakes is terrible.

☹ My emotions can't be controlled.

☹ I must never show any weakness.

☹ People must love/like me or I will be miserable.

☹ There is a perfect solution.

☹ People who are healthy do not get upset.

☹ I can do anything if I am in the mood.

☹ I should be happy all the time.

☹ Working on my problems could cause me more problems.

☹ You can't tell me anything about myself that I don't know.

☹ I am inferior.

☹ I should never hurt anyone.

☹ I can't change what I think.

Look at the list and evaluate yourself:

● Can you identify with any of these statements? Can you add any of your own thoughts that cause problems?

● Ask yourself how these things could prevent effective and legitimate assertion.

● Do you want to keep these beliefs in place or do you want to change them?

Personal Diary

ASSESSING YOURSELF
WHAT NOW IN COUNSELLING?

If you have followed this course consecutively you are now nearing the end of a personal journey into the field of counselling and communication. As with all endings the question is 'Where do I go next?'

This book does not claim to make you a counsellor or to qualify you in any way for the helping process. It is an introduction to many of the skills and issues which counsellors must know and acquire if they are to be effective helpers.

Some of you will now no doubt think that enough and perhaps too much has already been done! In which case you need go no further. My hope is that this book has given you some new thoughts, areas of exploration and opportunity for thinking about how you set about helping others and yourself. In which case this last chapter will give you the opportunity to assess overall your own performance and your own preference for counselling.

Others of you will feel that you want to go further and this unit aims to give you information which may help you in the ongoing process of becoming more skilled and more experienced.

✔ AIMS

Our aims in this unit are:

- To provide a checklist of important skills outlined in this manual.

- To give you an opportunity to assess your ongoing involvement in counselling.

- To give useful names and addresses of key institutes for training counsellors.

- To give you access to a short selected bibliography for further reading and resourcing.

STARTER ACTIVITY (10–15 MINS)

COUNSELLING: WHERE DO I GO FROM HERE?

Get into groups of two or three people. Individually, look at the list below and select which of these responses is closest to your own. You may wish to add a further category which is not mentioned. Discuss in your group how you see yourself at this stage in relation to being a counsellor.

☺ **I am still interested in counselling but I would need a lot more training and practice to feel that I can offer my services to anybody in need.**

☹ **I don't think I know myself well enough to avoid some of the complexities of counselling someone else—there is a lot of work to be done on myself first.**

☺ **I feel increasingly that I am called to counsel others but I still need further training.**

☺ **I think I am naturally inclined to counselling and I already feel equipped to do this.**

☺ **I am undecided. I don't think I am any good at this yet; others disagree with me.**

☺ I don't think counselling is for me.

☺ Other ....

GROUP ACTIVITY 1 (15–20 MINS)

ASSESSING AND COMMENTING ON YOUR OWN PERSONAL DEVELOPMENT DURING THIS COURSE
Below you will find a brief outline of the different modules in this book which follow the introductory Module 1. Referring back to your personal reflection notes and taking your time, go through the various units and give yourself a score from 1 to 5 on where you now think your skill lies:

1 = Non-effective

2 = Little skill

3 = A degree of competence

4 = A good working skill

5 = A high level of competence

CONTACT POINTS FOR FUTURE REFERENCE

For those of you who are thinking of training further or who would just like more information about what is available, there follow some useful names and addresses. Most of the forms of therapy cited have been referred to in the course you have just

---

Evaluation of course units

Module 2: Preparing to be a counsellor

Unit 2.1 Know yourself: what you bring to counselling	1 2 3 4 5
Unit 2.2 Communication and miscommunication	1 2 3 4 5
Unit 2.3 How to start: the first counselling appointment	1 2 3 4 5

Module 3: Discerning what others are saying

Unit 3.1 Exploring guilt and blame: the work of J. B. Rotter	1 2 3 4 5
Unit 3.2 Learning to forgive others and yourself	1 2 3 4 5
Unit 3.3 Listening and paraphrasing: two ways of showing care	1 2 3 4 5

Module 4: Learning to identify and express feelings

Unit 4.1 Reflecting feelings: the art of identifying feelings	1 2 3 4 5
Unit 4.2 Expressing feelings: the art of expressing emotion	1 2 3 4 5
Unit 4.3 Personality types: a resource for counsellors	1 2 3 4 5

Module 5: Skills of observation, confrontation and self-disclosure

Unit 5.1 The art of observation: non-verbal communication	1 2 3 4 5
Unit 5.2 The art of creative confrontation	1 2 3 4 5
Unit 5.3 The skill of self-disclosure	1 2 3 4 5

Module 6: Setting counselling and communication goals

Unit 6.1 Skills survey: assessing personal strengths and weaknesses	1 2 3 4 5
Unit 6.2 The skills of self-confidence and assertion	1 2 3 4 5
Unit 6.3 Assessing yourself: what now in counselling?	1 2 3 4 5

followed. You may of course find that, in the time it takes for this book to be published and for it to find its way into your hands, the addresses may have changed, but at least you will know who to ask directory enquiries for.

ADLERIAN THERAPY

THERAPY AND TRAINING
Adlerian Society for Individual Psychology
77 Clissold Crescent
London N16 9AR

BEHAVIOUR THERAPY

THERAPY AND TRAINING
Psychological Treatment Unit
Maudsley Hospital
London SE5

GESTALT THERAPY

THERAPY AND TRAINING
The Gestalt Centre, London
Administrator
64 Warwick Road
St Albans
Hertfordshire AL1 4DL

The Gestalt Psychotherapy
Training Institute UK
PO Box 620
Bristol BS99 7DL

PERSON-CENTRED THERAPY

THERAPY
Norwich Centre for Personal and
Professional Development
7 Earlham Road
Norwich NR2 3RA

PSYCHODYNAMIC THERAPY: THE FREUDIAN APPROACH
London Centre for Psychotherapy
19 Fitzjohn's Avenue
London NW3 5JY

TRAINING
British Association for Psychotherapy
121 Hendon Lane
London NW3 3PR

PSYCHODYNAMIC THERAPY: THE JUNGIAN APPROACH

THERAPY AND TRAINING
Society of Analytical Psychology
1 Daleham Gardens
London NW3 5BY

Association of Jungian Analysts
Flat 3, 7 Eton Avenue
London NW3 3EL

TRAINING
Facilitator Development Institute
(Address as above)

TRANSACTIONAL ANALYSIS

THERAPY AND TRAINING
Institute of Transactional Analysis
BM Box 4104
London WC1

FURTHER INFORMATION
Useful directories are available for training
and reference from:

British Association for Counselling
37A Sheep Street
Rugby
Warwickshire CV21 3BX

FEEDBACK

The author would welcome feedback on this training book. Also, if you are interested in day/short courses in either counselling, personality types or learning styles, correspondence should be addressed to:

Ms Linda Edwards (writing name is Smith)
Centre for Educational Studies
King's College London
Cornwall House Annexe
Waterloo Road
London SE1 8TX

COUNSELLING AND PSYCHOTHERAPY IN BRITAIN

At the time of writing, anyone in Britain can practise as a counsellor or psychotherapist. It may seem very strange to some readers that something as important as human development and personal change is not seen as a regulated profession. Neither is there any formal need for training nor, as in the case of the medical profession, subscription to a code of ethics. There are, however, changes ahead and it is expected that greater centralization of standards of practice will soon be implemented.

However, in the private sector, ordinary people have little protection against the charlatan, untrained or unethical therapist. There have been several attempts to regulate the profession of psychotherapy. In 1971, a government-appointed inquiry resulted in the Foster Report, which recommended regulation by statute. In 1978, the Sieghart Report proposed the establishment of a council which would enforce a code of professional ethics and help to approve training. Since then a private member's bill in parliament has failed and the core professionals have, sadly, been unable to agree on common ground. It is possible that the British Association for Counselling will become a registering body.

The lack of a central regulating body raises the issues of what constitutes competence and good practice. This is very important for every individual who is a practising counsellor because everyone tends to work in relative isolation and, unless there is ongoing training, poor practice may go unheeded.

Learning to heal and to help human beings is a lifelong process and I am fully aware that this training book has only just touched the surface. There is so much that needs to follow to make the training complete. But my hope and prayer is that it may have given you the opportunity to take the next step in a spiritual journey—the journey into knowing and healing ourselves and others. For those of you who feel called to counsel, may he—the Holy Spirit, the Counsellor—show you all things, and lead you into all truth.

BIBLIOGRAPHY

Adler, A., *The Neurotic Constitution*, Kegan Paul, Tench, Trubner & Co., London, 1912

Adler, A., *Understanding Human Nature*, Allen & Unwin, London, 1927

Adler, A., *The Practice and Theory of Individual Psychology*, Routledge & Kegan Paul, 1929

Adler, A., *Social Interest: A Challenge to Mankind*, Faber & Faber, London, 1933

Argyle, M., *The Psychology of Interpersonal Behaviour* (4th edn), Penguin, Harmondsworth, 1983

Argyle, M., *Social Interaction*, Methuen, London, 1969

Argyle, M., *Social Skill and Mental Health*, Bryant & Trower

Berne E., *Games People Play*, Penguin, Harmondsworth, 1964

Berne, E., *Transactional Analysis in Psychotherapy: A Systematic Individual and Social Psychiatry*, Souvenir Press, London, 1975

Briggs-Myers, I., *Gifts Differing*, Consulting Psychologist Press, Palo Alto, Calif., 1980

Brown, D. and Pedder, J., *Introduction to Psychotherapy*, Tavistock, 1979

Butler, P. E., *Self-Assertion for Women*, Harper & Row, New York, 1981

Carr, Wesley, *The Pastor as Theologian*, SPCK, 1989

Dryden, W. (ed.), *Individual Therapy: A Handbook*, Open University Press, Milton Keynes, 1990

Egan, G., *The Skilled Helper*, Brooks-Cole Publishing, United States, 1975

Fordham, F., *An Introduction to Jung's Psychology*, Penguin, Harmondsworth, 1979

Freud, S., *The Interpretation of Dreams*, SE 4 and 5:1–626, 1900

Freud, S., *On the Sexual Theories of Children*, SE 9:205–26, 1908

Freud, S., *The Unconscious*, SE 14:159–209, 1915

Fromm, E., *Psychoanalysis and Religion*, Yale University Press, 1950

Hammond, John et al., *New Methods in Religious Education Teaching—An Experimental Approach*, Olwer & Boyd, 1990

Harris, T., *I'm O.K. You're O.K*, Pan Books, London, 1973

Hillman, J., *Archetypal Psychology: A Brief Account*, Spring, Dallas, 1983

Hurding, R., *Roots and Shoots—A Guide to Counselling and Psychotherapy*, Hodder & Stoughton, London, 1986

Jacobs, M., *Swift to Hear*, SPCK, 1985

Jourard, S., *The Transparent Self*, Van Nostrand, 1964

Jung, C., *Memories, Dreams and Reflections*, recorded and edited by Aniela Jaffé, Pantheon Books, New York, 1963

Jung, C. G., *Psychological Types*, Collected Works 6, Routledge & Kegan Paul, London, 1971

Jung, C. G., *The Collected Works*, edited by Read, H., Fordham, M., Adler, G., and McGuire, W., translated in the main by Hull, R., London, Routledge & Kegan Paul/ Princeton University Press

Kaufmann, W., *Discovering the Mind*, Volume 3: 'Freud vs Adler and Jung', McGraw-Hill, New York, 1980

Kraft, C. H., *Communication Theory for Christian Witness*, Abingdon Press, Nashville, 1983

Leach, E., *Culture and Communication*, Cambridge University Press, Cambridge, 1976

Nelson-Jones, R., *The Theory and Practice of Counselling Psychology*, Holt, Rinehart & Winston, London, 1982

Nelson-Jones, R., *Practical Counselling and Helping Skills*, Cassell Educational Ltd, 1993

Perls, F. S., *Gestalt Therapy*, Dell, New York, 1951

Perls, F. S., Hefferline, R. F. and Goodman, P., *Gestalt Therapy*, Penguin, Harmondsworth, 1974

Rogers, C. R., *Client-Centred Therapy*, Houghton Mifflin, Boston, Mass, 1951

Rogers, C. R., *Counseling and Psychotherapy*, Houghton Mifflin, Boston, Mass, 1942

Rogers, C. R., *On Becoming a Person*, Houghton Mifflin, Boston, Mass, 1961

Rotter, J. B., *Social Learning and Clinical Psychology*, Prentice-Hall, Englewood Cliffs H.J., 1954

Seligman, M. E. P., *Helplessness*, Freeman, San Francisco, Calif., 1975

Sharp, D., *Personality Types: Jung's Model of Typology*, Inner City Books, Toronto, Canada, 1987

Skinner, B. F., *Beyond Freedom and Dignity*, Penguin, Harmondsworth, 1973

The Secret of the Golden Flower: A Chinese Book of Life, translated and explained by Richard Wilhelm with a commentary by C. G. Jung, Harcourt, Brace & World, New York, 1965

Vitz, P. C., *Psychology as Religion: The Cult of Self Worship*, Lion, Oxford, 1977

NOTES

NOTES

NOTES

NOTES